THE BRITISH LIBRARY

The Reference Division Collections

CONTENTS

ES nouuelles dalbyon
Sil bous en plaust escouter
mon frere z mon compaignon
Sachez qua mon retourner
Ay este deça la mer
E ceu a joyeuse chiere

THE BRITISH LIBRARY
REFERENCE DIVISION

THE BIRTH OF THE LIBRARY

The British Library was established by Act of Parliament in 1973. It has three main divisions, the Lending Division, the Bibliographic Services Division, and the Reference Division. There are also a Research and Development Department and a Central Administration.

The Reference Division is the one with which readers and the general public are the most familiar, for it was formed in the main from the library departments of the British Museum – that is, the Department of Printed Books, the Department of Manuscripts, the Department of Oriental Printed Books and Manuscripts and the National Reference Library for Science and Invention (now the Science Reference Library).

The holdings of these departments, which today number more than 10 million volumes, began as three collections of manuscripts, books and other materials whose acquisition by the state in the 18th century led directly to the establishment of the British Museum, by the British Museum Act of 1753.

Thus, although the British Library has been in existence for just one decade, the Reference Division can trace its origins back more than two and a quarter centuries to the foundation of the British Museum.

The 1753 Act provided for the safe preservation of the three collections in the care of a board of Trustees 'for publick use to all Posterity' – a phrase which neatly encapsulates the main aims and functions of today's Library. The Act also effectively created the first state library accessible to the public in Britain, for at this time there was no equivalent of the modern public library. In providing a Reading Room where the materials in its keeping could be studied free by 'all studious and curious Persons', as the 1753 Act put it, the new British Museum took the first steps towards filling the gap.

The three foundation collections of books and manuscripts in the British Museum's Library departments were all made by individual collectors. Foremost among them, because it was the bequeathing of his collections to the nation which was the spur to the establishment of the British Museum, was Sir Hans Sloane.

A miniature of the White Tower of the Tower of London with London Bridge in the background, from a manuscript, c. 1500, of the poems of Charles d'Orleans who was captured at Agincourt in 1415 and remained a prisoner in England until 1440. 36.5cm × 27cm
Royal MS 16 F ii, f. 73

3

This physician, amateur scientist, antiquarian and President of the Royal Society built up collections of natural history, geological, zoological and medical phenomena, antiquities from Greece, Rome, Egypt and the Orient, drawings, coins and medals, and many books and manuscripts whose value and importance were recognised in his own lifetime. When Sir Hans died in 1753, aged 92, he bequeathed his collections to the nation, provided that his daughters were paid £20,000.

The government accepted the bequest, deciding to house it with another state-owned collection, the Cotton collection of medieval manuscripts, cartularies, state papers and antiquities, whose importance may be judged from the fact that it counted among its treasures the *Lindisfarne Gospels*, two copies of *Magna Carta*, and the manuscript of *Beowulf*. This collection was made by Sir Robert Cotton during the reigns of Elizabeth I and James I and was donated to the state in 1700 'for publick use and advantage' by Sir Robert's grandson, Sir John Cotton, but had not been available to scholars for many years.

At the same time, the government also bought the Harleian collection of manuscripts, charters and rolls made by Robert Harley, first Earl of Oxford and one-time chief minister to Queen Anne, and his son, Edward, the second Earl.

By the time the British Museum, housed in Montagu House, a former ducal mansion in Bloomsbury, opened in 1759, a fourth important collection had been added to the first three. This was the old Royal Library (so-called to distinguish it from the library collected by George III, most of which also found its way into the British Museum), which was begun in the 1470s by Edward IV, added to by succeeding monarchs, and given to the Museum by George II in 1757.

This magnificent gift brought to the Museum thousands of manuscripts and printed books, including such items as the fifth-century Greek biblical manuscript, the *Codex Alexandrinus*. It also brought the Museum the important right of copyright deposit, under an Act of 1709 which had provided that the Royal Library should receive one copy of every printed work registered at Stationers' Hall. Although little used until the mid-19th century, this provision was to be a major contributor to the growth of the Museum's library departments.

The gift of the Royal Library established a precedent for bequests and donations which has brought the Museum and Library many valuable items over the years. In the early years, collections came from people as diverse in their interests as the actor David Garrick, the music historian Charles Burney, the naturalist Sir Joseph Banks, and the former Member of Parliament Thomas Grenville. The tradition continues today, though considerably reduced as a source of acquisitions, owing to the burden of taxation.

The new British Museum had three departments, Manuscripts, Printed Books, and Natural and Artificial Productions, and its chief officer was the Principal Librarian. This position was the only one specifically mentioned in the British Museum Act, and reflected the importance of the books and manuscripts in the Museum's keeping. The title was to remain unchanged until 1898, when 'and Director' was added to it.

Services for readers, who were comparatively few until the early 19th century, developed steadily. The Reading Room was moved several times, the present round and domed Reading Room, which was opened in 1857, being the Museum's seventh.

This Reading Room was, in fact, in a new building, for the British Museum had long-since outgrown Montagu House. As early as 1806 a new gallery had been needed to house the Townley collection of classical art. In 1823, when George IV offered to the Museum most of the new Royal Library amassed during the long lifetime of his father, George III, there was nowhere to put this important collection. The Trustees had to approach Parliament, which voted £40,000 for the

The Reading Room, shortly after it was opened in 1857.

The end of St John's Gospel in the Codex Sinaiticus, one of the two earliest complete Bibles. Written in Greek by three scribes in the middle of the 4th century, it has since lost half its Old Testament. The discovery of the Codex Sinaiticus in the 19th century revolutionised the study of the text of the New Testament. 38cm × 34.5cm

Add. MS. 43725, f. 260

The unique manuscript of the epic Anglo-Saxon poem, Beowulf, the oldest epic in the English language. This copy, made *c*. AD 1000, was written as prose, without division of lines. The manuscript was among those damaged in the Cotton Library fire of 1731. 21cm × 14.3cm

Cotton MS Vitellius A xv, f. 132

A papyrus letter, in Greek, from the third century BC, written by Epharmostos to his brother Zenon, agent to the royal finance minister in Philadelphia, complaining 'Your last letter was eaten by mice.' 9cm × 12.9cm

Papyrus 2655

building of a new east wing, which still houses the King's Library, transferred from Buckingham Palace in 1828. Eventually, Montagu House was demolished and a new museum was built to designs by Robert (later Sir Robert) Smirke whose elegantly classical building included the colonnaded portico which is still, surely, the most memorable feature of the Great Russell Street entrance to the British Museum.

Under reforms initiated by Antonio Panizzi (later Sir Anthony Panizzi), Keeper of Printed Books from 1837 and Principal Librarian from 1856 to 1866, the Museum was transformed into a great cultural repository and the library departments became in fact, if not yet in name, the national library of Britain.

Specialist collections, such as those of maps, music and official papers, grew rapidly in the second half of the 19th century, and public exhibitions of items from the library collections became a permanent feature of the Grenville and King's Libraries. Firm implementation of the 1842 Copyright Act also meant that printed material now came into the British Museum's library departments in enormous quantities from Great Britain, while the expansion of Empire brought even more material from all parts of the world. All this material was housed on the Bloomsbury site. Although the Newspaper Collection was given its own library at Colindale in north London in the 1930s, it was not until the passing of the 1963 Act which modernised the Museum's

One of the four surviving exemplifications of the text of Magna Carta issued by King John at Runnymede in June 1215. The British Library has two of the surviving originals, and the others are in the archives of Lincoln and Salisbury Cathedrals.
34.5cm × 51.3cm
Cotton MS Augustus II. 106

administration that the library departments were enabled to out-house large parts of their collections, particularly of printed books, and to lend items to other museums and galleries.

An important advance in the quality of the service the library departments offered their readers was the publication of a printed catalogue during the latter part of the 19th century. Before this, the General Catalogue was available only in unwieldy manuscript form. A Subject Index was also issued.

The 20th century has seen a continuing growth in the library departments of the British Museum, despite the hazards of two world wars. In 1960 the British Museum was given responsibility for creating the National Reference Library for Science and Invention by taking over and expanding the Patent Office Library, one of the country's leading science and technology libraries founded in 1855. The most far-reaching development of recent years has been the establishment of the national British Library, in which the former library departments of the Museum make up the major part of the Reference Division. A new department was added to the Division in 1982 when responsibility for the administration of the India Office Library and Records was transferred from the Foreign and Commonwealth Office to the Board of the British Library.

Although the Division has otherwise entirely severed its two-centuries-long connection with the Museum, it still has its main home in the Bloomsbury building, and is likely to continue to occupy parts of it until its own building in Euston Road just west of St Pancras Station should be ready for occupation.

Constant growth has meant that not all sections of the Reference Division have been able to remain on the main Bloomsbury site. The Department of Oriental Manuscripts and Printed Books and its Reading Room are in Store Street, and the India Office Library and Records are in Blackfriars Road. The Science Reference Library is still housed in the Patent Office in Southampton Buildings and in five other buildings in central London; the Newspaper Library is at Colindale in north London, and there are other buildings and stores in London, most notably at Woolwich.

THE REFERENCE DIVISION TODAY

Within the British Library, the Reference Division has a dual role as 'book museum' and one of the world's most important reference libraries, with resources ranging over all civilizations, every age and every subject.

Its role as a museum of the book may be seen in its exhibition galleries: the Grenville Library, Manuscript Saloon, King's Library, Crawford Room and Map Gallery, all in the east wing of the British Museum. Here are displayed many of the Library's best-known

è possibile che ~~chi della spechio~~ ~~chonsperica possa~~ che tan
to quanto il sole allumina
dello spechio sperichο tan
to desso spechio ab
bia a risplendere
sega esso spechio
non fussi ochato
a globbulo

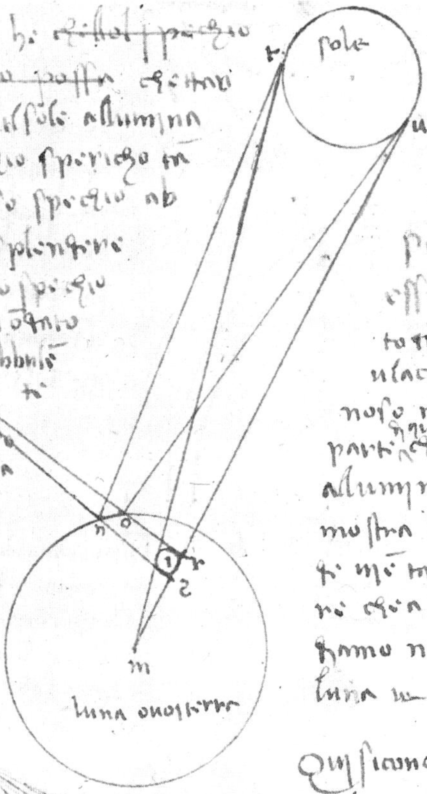

Alla luna alluminata dal so
sole la luna da sé p
chè non risplende sanza
l'aiuto del sole. E la
luna alluminata dal so
le ma fa spechio sperico
e se lli è spechio non è proba
to in prospectiva che'l sim
ulacro d'uno obbietto lumi
noso non sarà mai equale alla
parte che in esso luminoso he (di quello spechio)
alluminato) e se così come
mostra qui la figura in r 2 detto
di mē tanta quantita di splendo
re che a il plenilunio che noi ve
diamo nella quinta decima della
luna

vedi qui il so
le allumina
re la luna
chome speri
cho e tan
to quanto il
so sole ne
ue di tanto
fa splēdere

Qui si conclude che ciò che della luna
splende e acqua simile a quella de
li nostri mari e così in tutta e cau
che lei non risplende sono il sole e tter
ra ferma

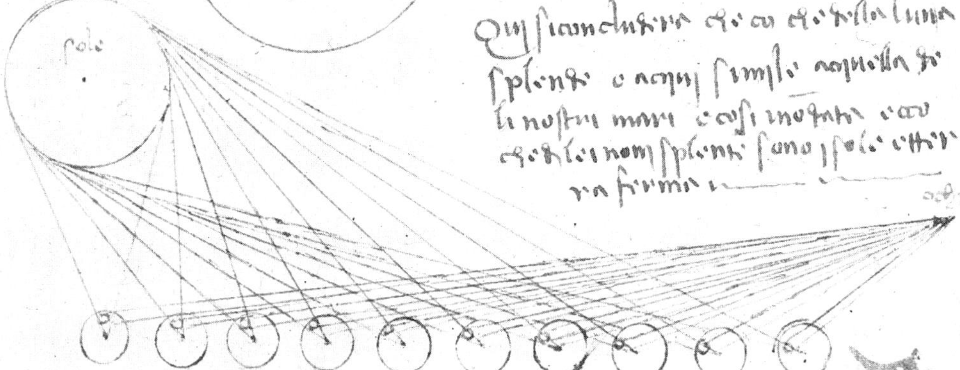

Questa dimostratione di vari corpi sperichi interposti infra l'ochio
e il sole ~~no~~ è fatta p mostrare ~~che~~ che siccome ~~e~~ in ciascuno d'essi
corpi si vede il simulacro del sole così si po vedere esso simulacro in ci
scuna globbosita delle onde del mare e come in molti di questi sperici si
vede molti soli così in molte onde si vede molti lustri li quali in molta
distanzia ciascun lustro p se si fa grande all'ochio e così facendo ciascu
na onda si vengono a congiugnere le sue parti interposte infra l'onde e
per questa tal cagione e pare tutto un sole continuato nelli molti soli
spechiati nelle molte onde e le parti onde misti colle sperici luminose
fan che tutto splendore non è lucido come quel del sole in esso di spechia
to

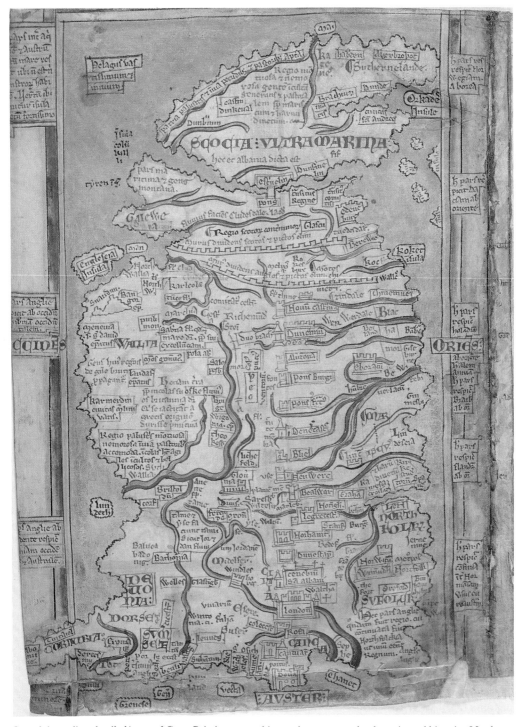

One of the earliest detailed maps of Great Britain extant, this was drawn *c.* 1250 by the artist and historian Matthew Paris, a monk of St Albans. Noticeable features are the Roman walls dividing England and Scotland.
33.5cm × 24.5cm

Cotton MS Claudius D VI, f. 12b

Opposite: A page of notes on the sun and moon from a notebook of Leonardo da Vinci (1452–1519), partly written at Florence in 1508 and mainly concerned with dynamics. The text, in Italian, is in 'mirror writing,' written left-handed from right to left in reversed letters. 21cm × 14.3cm

Arundel MS 263, f. 28b

treasures, including the *Diamond Sutra, Magna Carta*, a Shakespeare First Folio, the *Lindisfarne Gospels*, the *Bedford Hours* and an autograph preliminary version of *Alice's Adventures in Wonderland* as well as many less familiar, though no less interesting items. Special exhibitions, which form an important part of the Reference Division's services to its general visitors, are also mounted in these galleries. Lectures and illustrated talks in the galleries or in the Seminar Room are provided by the Library's Education Service.

The Reference Division's other, major role within the British Library involves it in a much wider world than that enclosed in the book-lined walls of the exhibition galleries.

The British Library is the national centre of reference, study, bibliographical and other information services and, within this context, the Reference Division's main task is to make available to readers and scholars and researchers as much as possible of the vast range of resources at its disposal. These resources are in the care of five departments within the Division. The Department of Printed Books, which includes the Map, Music, Newspaper and Official Publications Libraries and the Philatelic Collection, has 8,750,000 volumes which are consulted in its various reading rooms by over half a million readers every year. The Department of Manuscripts includes among its 100,000 volumes items as diverse as the *Codex Sinaiticus*, one of the earliest and most important manuscripts of the Bible, and letters from novelists or poets to their friends. The Department of Oriental Manuscripts and Printed Books has half a million manuscripts and printed books whose contents cover all the literary languages of Asia and North and North-East Africa. As part of its intensive collection of worldwide scientific and technological literature the Science Reference Library holds more than 20 million patent specifications including every one registered in Britain since 1617, and the India Office Library and Records, which developed from the activities of the East India Company, holds one of the world's largest reference and archival collections concerned mainly, though not entirely, with South Asia.

The Library's collections are constantly added to by acquisition, gift and exchange, much of it at international government and institution level, though its specialist staffs also maintain their own contacts and supply links at home and abroad. In any one year, the Reference Division may register the acquisition of literally millions of items – 2,100,000 in 1979–80, for instance – including many thousands of issues of journals and other serial publications, patents, newspapers, atlases and map sheets as well as books and manuscripts, usually including ones of great rarity.

Not a few important acquisitions come from itself, for the Division is a publisher in its own right, publishing under the imprint of The British Library. Specialist catalogues are major items in the list, which also includes important works of scholarship by members of the

Above: Sewing a headband on a volume under repair in the British Library Bindery
(Crown Copyright)

Below: Retouching a vellum document, in the British Library Bindery
(Crown Copyright)

Division's staff, and books and guides associated with the Reference Division's constantly changing programme of special exhibitions.

While the Reference Division's immediate responsibility is to those readers who come in person to its five departments in search of information, it also maintains a correspondence with libraries, institutions and individual scholars all over the world. Just as an increasing amount of new material comes into the Division in microform, so the forms of many of its services to its readers have been radically altered by its use of the most up-to-date advances in computer technology, microforms and other aspects of Information Technology.

Both readers coming to the reading rooms and correspondents abroad can obtain microfilm and photocopy versions of original material and wide-ranging computer search facilities are available covering reference collections in the UK and abroad. Additions to the catalogues of the Department of Printed Books have been produced in Computer Output Microfilm since 1975; although the cost of putting all its holdings on photo-microform seems prohibitive, the Reference Division has in hand the conversion of the vast General Catalogue to machine-readable form.

The King's Library, completed in 1828, still houses the magnificent library collected by King George III. The statue on the right is William Shakespeare, by L. F. Roubiliac.

Scientific research and advanced technology also play their parts in the constant work of conservation and restoration carried on in the Division's conservation sections, where many thousands of volumes and individual items must be treated every year if the Division's holdings are to be preserved intact for future generations of users.

Incipit prologus sancti iheronimi presbiteri in parabolas salomonis.

Iungat epistola quos iungit sacerdotium: immo carta non diuidat: quos xpi nectit amor. Comentarios in osee. amos. 7 zachariam malachiam quoq; poscitis. Scripsisse: si licuisset pre valitudine. Mittitis solacia sumptuum. notarios nros et librarios sustentaris: ut vobis potissimum nrm desudet ingenium. Et ecce ex latere frequens turba diuersa poscentium: quasi aut equum sit me vobis esurientibus aliis laborare: aut in ratione dati et accepti cuiquam preter vos obnoxius sim. Itaq; longa egrotatione fractus: ne penitus hoc anno reticerem 7 apud vos mutus essem: tridui opus nomini vro consecraui: interpretatione videlicet trium salomonis voluminum: malloth qd hebrei pabolas. vulgata editio puibia vocat: coeleth quem grece eccliasten: latine ocionatorem possum dicere: sirasirim qd in linguam nram vertit canticum canticorum. Fertur et panaretos: ihu filii sirach liber: 7 alius pseudographus qui sapientia salomonis inscribit. Quorum priorem hebraicum reperi: non eccliasticum ut apud latinos: sed pabolas pnotatum. Cui iuncti erant eccliastes: et canticu canticorum: ut similitudine salomonis: non solum numero librorum: sed etiam materiarum genere coequaret. Secundus apud hebreos nusq; est: quia et ipse stilus grecam eloquentiam redolet: et nonnulli scriptorum veteres hunc esse iudei filonis affirmant. Sicut ergo iudith 7 thobie 7 machabeorum libros: legit quidem eos ecclia: sed inter canonicas scripturas non recipit: sic 7 hec duo volumina legat ad edificatione plebis: non ad auctoritatem ecclesiasticorum dogmatum affirmandam.

Si cui sane septuaginta interpretum magis editio placet: habet eam a nobis olim emendatam. Neq; enim noua sic cudimus: ut vetera destruamus. Et tamen cum diligentissime legerit: sciat magis nra scripta intelligi: que non in tercium vas transfusa coacuerit: sed statim de prelo purissime comendata teste: suum saporem seruauerit. Incipiut parabole salomonis.

Parabole salomonis filii dauid regis isrl: ad sciendam sapientiam 7 disciplinam: ad intelligenda verba prudentie et suscipienda eruditione doctrine: iusticiam et iudicium 7 equitatem: ut detur paruulis astucia: et adolescenti scientia et intellectus. Audiens sapiens sapientior erit: 7 intelliges gubernacla possidebit. Animaduertet parabolam et interpretationem: verba sapientium 7 enigmata eorum. Timor dni principium sapientie. Sapientiam atq; doctrinam stulti despiciunt. Audi fili mi disciplinam patris tui et ne dimittas legem matris tue: ut addatur gracia capiti tuo: 7 torques collo tuo. Fili mi si te lactauerint peccatores: ne acquiescas eis. Si dixerint veni nobiscum insidiemur sanguini: abscondamus tendiculas contra insontem frustra: deglutiamus eum sicud infernus viuentem 7 integrum: quasi descendentem in lacum: omnem preciosam substantiam reperiemus: implebimus domus nras spoliis: sortem mitte nobiscum: marsupium sit vnum omnium nrm: fili mi ne ambules cum eis. Prohibe pedem tuum a semitis eorum. Pedes enim illorum ad malum currunt: 7 festinant ut effundant sanguinem. Frustra autem iacitur rete ante oculos pennatorum. Ipsi quoq; contra sanguinem suum insidiantur: et

DEPARTMENT OF
PRINTED BOOKS

The Department of Printed Books is the largest in the Reference Division and was one of the three original departments of the British Museum. Its collection of around 8,500,000 volumes has its origins in the early collections of the museums – the Sloane Library, the old Royal Library and the King's Library – and includes books, periodicals and newspapers, atlases, maps, music scores and stamps, as well as such related items as globes, book bindings, sales catalogues and newspaper clippings. More than 600,000 new items are acquired annually. Many items are then bound together into volumes.

The number of people who use the Department's services may also be counted by the million, for in addition to the half million or so visits made to the Department's various reading rooms every year, staff help many more than this via its postal, telecommunication and computer search services.

Within the Department of Printed Books there are several separate subject collections or libraries with their own catalogues, reading rooms (or reading areas) and other specialist services for readers. These are the Map Library, Music Library, Newspaper Library, Official Publications Library and Philatelic Collection. The Library Association Library, an extensive specialist reference collection of librarian-ship and information science, housed in the Library Association building in Ridgmount Street, is also part of the British Library within the Department of Printed Books.

The British Library's famous domed Reading Room, with the North Library adjoining it, is the main focus of the Department's service to the public. The Reading Room was opened in 1857 (see p. 5) and the galleried North Library was built just before 1914, connecting the main museum building and the Reading Room with the new King Edward VII Building.

The great bulk of the Printed Books Department's holdings have come to it under the legal regulations requiring the deposit with the Library of one copy of all printed material published in the United Kingdom, and through the systematic purchase since the 1830s of overseas literature. In recent years particularly, intergovernmental exchange of official publications has become a major source of supply of newly published literature. Gifts and donations, including entire

A page from the Gutenberg Bible, or the 42-line Bible. This Bible in Latin was the first book ever printed from movable type. It was printed in Mainz, c. 1455 by Johann Gutenberg, Johann Fust and Peter Schoeffer.

C. 9. d. 4

libraries collected by individuals, have also brought the Department many rare and important items.

The Sloane Library, the old Royal Library and the King's Library, still housed in the east wing built to receive it in 1828, are outstanding among the individual libraries in the collections. The importance of the book part of the Sloane Library to the new Department of Printed Books lay not so much in its possession of rare items as in its size and the wide-ranging nature of its contents; it formed, in fact, the bulk of the collections for several decades. The old Royal Library, though largely consisting of manuscripts, also brought a wealth of printed books including several volumes showing annotations in royal hands. The King's Library, amassed by and for George III, included a fine collection of incunabula and many other books of antiquarian interest as well as the standard works of the day. The geographical and topographical elements of this library were also large and of considerable importance, including maps, charts, prints and drawings.

Another important private library inherited by the Department is the library collected by a Whig Member of Parliament, Thomas Grenville; it now lines the walls of the Grenville Library.

Among the treasures contained in the Grenville Library are rare editions of Homer and Aesop, the Girardot de Préfond copy of the 42-line Bible, the unique complete, two-volume copy of Azzoguidi's first edition of Ovid, printed in Bologna in 1471, the British Library's only copy of the Mainz Psalter of 1457, and fourteen books printed by Caxton.

Above left: A page from Geoffrey Chaucer's *The Canterbury Tales*, the first major book printed in England by Caxton, which was printed at Westminster in 1476
167.c.26

Above right: William Tyndale, assisted by William Roy, made the first translation into English of the New Testament. This page of the Gospel of St Matthew is from Tyndale's Bible, printed in Cologne by P. Quentell in 1525.
G. 12179

Below left: A famous example of Roman type in Francesco Colonna's *Hypnerotomachia Poliphili*, printed in Venice by Aldus Manutius in 1499. This book is renowned for the harmony of its type and woodcuts.

G. 10564

Below right: The opening words of *The Canterbury Tales*, from an edition of the Works of Geoffrey Chaucer printed by the Kelmscott Press, Hammersmith, 1896. The woodcuts were designed by Sir Edward Burne-Jones, and the borders, initials and ornaments by William Morris.

C. 43. h. 19

Four collections which preceded the arrival of the Grenville Library in the British Museum indicate, in the contrasting nature of their subjects, the wide-ranging quality of the Printed Books collection.

The earliest of the four to be acquired was the 4,500 rare and fine volumes collected by the Rev. Clayton Mordaunt Cracherode, one of the great bibliophiles of the latter half of the 18th century. When he died in 1799 he bequeathed almost the whole of his collections of books, coins and prints (whose acquisition had occupied most of his life) to the British Museum, of which he was a Trustee.

In great contrast to the Cracherode books, which were distinguished as much for their beauty as for their contents, were the contents of the three Croker French Revolution Tract collections of periodicals published during the French Revolution. The first collection was made chiefly by Marat's publisher, Colin, and was bought by the Museum in 1817 on the advice of John Wilson Croker, a leading English authority on the Revolution. Croker himself collected the other two series of French Revolution tracts, which he sold to the Museum in 1831 and 1856.

Quite different again in its subject matter and style was the Banks

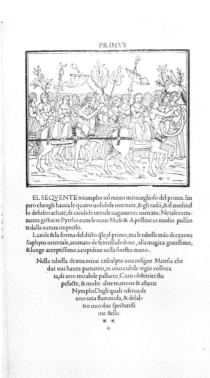

Eie begynneth the volume intituled and named
The recuyell of the hiftoryes of Troye compoſed
and drawen out of dyverſe bookes of latyn in
to frenſſhe by the ryght venerable perſone and woꝛ
ſhipfull man. Raoul le ffeure: prieſt and chapelayn
unto the ryght noble glozyous and myghty prynce in
his tyme Phelip duc of Bourgoyne of Brabande ꝛc
In the yere of the Incarnacion of our loꝛd god a thou
ſand foure hondeꝛd ſixty and foure / And tranſlated
and drawen out of frenſhe into engliſſhe by Wylliam
Caxton merceꝛ of ye cyte of London / at the comaundemet
of the right hye myghty and vertuouſe Prynceſſe hys
redoubtyd lady. Margarete by the grace of god. Du
cheſſe of Bourgoyne of Lotryk of Brabande ꝛc /
Whiche ſayd tranſlacion and werke was begonne in
Brugis in the Countee of Flaundres the fyrſt day of
marche the yere of the Incarnacion of our ſaid loꝛd god
a thouſand foure hondeꝛd ſixty and eyght / And ended
and fynyſſhid in the holy cyte of Coleyn the. xix. day of
ſeptembre the yere of our ſayd loꝛd god a thouſand
foure hondeꝛd ſixty and enleuen ꝛc.

And on that other ſide of this leef foloweth the prologe

Opposite: The fine binding of a *Book of Common Prayer*, London 1669. Made by Samuel Mearne, *c.* 1674, the binding is of gold-tooled red morocco with a cottage design painted in black and the cypher of King Charles II. The fore-edge is painted under the gold.

7. f. 13.

The Recuyell of the Historyes of Troyes, by Raoul Lefèvre, printed in Flanders (possibly Bruges) by William Caxton in 1473–4. This was the first book printed in English.

C. 11. C. 1.

ARMA:VIRVMQVE CANO:
troię qui primus ab oris
Italiam fato profugus:
lauinaꝗ uenit
L ittora:multum ille & terris iactatus:& alto
V i ſuperum:ſcꝗ memorem iunonis ob iram.

The opening words of the *Aeneid*, in the first dated edition of Virgil's Works, by Vindelinus de Spira, Venice, 1470

C. 6. c. 2

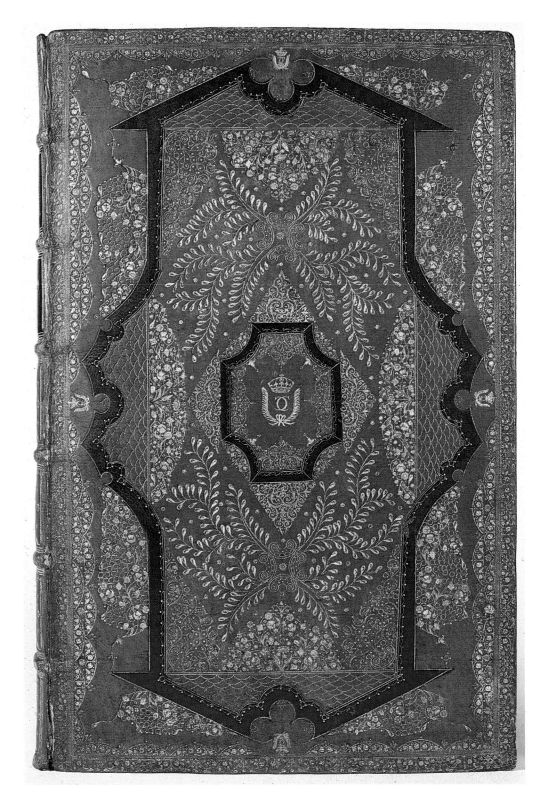

Library, collected by the botanist and zoologist, Sir Joseph Banks, who as a young man had accompanied Captain James Cook on his first voyage of exploration in the *Endeavour*. Banks bequeathed his large library, which included many books on travel and exploration as well as on botany and zoology, to his librarian, Robert Brown, with reversion to the British Museum. In fact, Brown passed the books on to the Museum in his own lifetime, and was given work space there so that he could continue to catalogue them.

Another library purchased around this time was that formed by Charles Burney, son of the music historian and brother of the novelist, Fanny Burney. Burney's library, which contained manuscripts as well as printed books, was particularly strong in the classical Greek and Latin authors. He also formed a collection of newspapers which is perhaps the most important source of 18th-century English newspapers still surviving.

Since then collections have continued to be added; the Huth collection (1906), the Ashley Library (1937), the Henry Davis gift of book bindings (1968), books from the Broxbourne Library (1976) and the nucleus of John Evelyn's Library (1977) are outstanding examples, most of which were generous gifts by benefactors. Today, the Department of Printed Books comprises one of the great collections of the world. While its basic tasks – acquisition, cataloguing, conservation and serving the public – have remained unchanged in more than two centuries, the ways in which it tackles these tasks have changed dramatically, especially in recent years.

Modern technology brings printed material into the Library in various forms other than traditional book format, notably microfilm. Because the originals are no longer obtainable, about half of the 250,000 volumes which were destroyed by bombing in World War II have been replaced by microfilm versions of copies held by other libraries.

The current Catalogue of works received in the Department since July 1975 and published in 1971 or later is produced on microfiches (each of which contains 208 two-column pages). There are two sequences, author/title and subject, and the catalogue is updated every two months. There are long-term proposals to put the entire General Catalogue (i.e. the catalogue of pre-1971 material already familiar in published editions) on to a computer file.

The computer gives readers new tools with which to search those parts of the Department's holdings which have been entered on the automated system. A computer search is an efficient way of obtaining information quickly, in the form of a convenient print-out; a simple search of a few seconds can replace days of looking through conventional printed catalogues.

An outstanding example of the use of computer technology is the Eighteenth-Century Short-Title Catalogue (ESTC) which became available through the British Library's on-line service, BLAISE-

Little Goody Two-Sh[

Oliver Goldsmith may have been the author of this anonymous *The History of Little Goody Two-Shoes*. This is the unique copy of the first edition, printed in London for J. Newbery in 1765.
C. 180. a. 3.

The title page, with a portrait of the playwright, of the First Folio edition of the collected plays of William Shakespeare. It was printed in London in 1623 by Isaac Iaggard and Ed. Blount.
G. 11631

Mr. WILLIAM
SHAKESPEARES

COMEDIES,
HISTORIES, &
TRAGEDIES.

Published according to the True Originall Copies.

Martin Droeshout sculpsit London.

LONDON
Printed by Iſaac Iaggard, and Ed. Blount. 1623.

Italian poster of the First World War

Comfortable and functional clothing for children, based on the theories of John Locke. Plate from *Journal des Luxus und der Moden*, Vol. II, Weimar 1787.

Opposite: *Mimosa Grandiflora*, a large flowering sensitive plant. Plate from R. Thornton, *Temple of Flora*, London 1807.

Fashion plate, by Gerda Wegener, from *Journal des Dames et des Modes*, Paris, July 1914.

23

LINE, in 1982. The ESTC at present comprises over 135,000 bibliographic records of books, pamphlets and many types of ephemera (i.e. leaflets etc.) printed in Britain and its colonies, and any item printed in English anywhere in the world between 1701 and 1800. It is thought that 10 per cent of the items on the files have never been recorded before. Recording of the data in ESTC took five years, and it is estimated that adding material from over 400 libraries throughout the world will take till the end of the 1980s.

The British Library's automated information service, BLAISE, holds bibliographic records created by the British Library and the Library of Congress in the United States. In addition, it provides links to many other databases at home and abroad. Thus, a reader in the Reading Room in London can request information which may come to him overnight from sources thousands of miles away.

Conserving the Printed Books collections for future generations accounts for a seventh of the annual expenditure of the whole Reference Division. The Department's problem is two-fold: how to repair the damage done by constant use and how to solve the basic problem of stopping wood-pulp paper deteriorating even as it sits on the shelves. It has been estimated that between 4 and 5 million books in the Library are printed on paper whose acid content leads to a serious risk of deterioration.

The Division has a large conservation staff, and the Library finances research programmes into various aspects of the treatment of papers and other materials aimed at halting or preventing decay and deterioration. Routine binding, re-binding and other conservation work is carried out in the Library's own binderies and by outside contractors at a rate of about 150,000 books a year.

The conservation programme is supplemented by a programme of systematic microfilming. This programme may lead to some form of optico-electronic system of data retrieval which would virtually eliminate the need for scholars to use original books at all. But to convert the millions of pages of information now in the Department's collections and then to keep up with current publications, must be a project for the uncertain and long-term future; most information about the past will continue to be taken from books in libraries of the traditional kind within the lifetime of everyone now living.

Whatever the role of the book in the future, there will remain an obligation on the Library to preserve the physical state of its collections as perfectly as possible for posterity. There is an inherent conflict between this duty and the duty to make them easily accessible to the readers of today; also there is a continuing challenge in trying to provide for the known needs of present-day readers, while at the same time trying to estimate and provide for the needs of the future. The resolution of these conflicting aims is the most important problem facing the Department of Printed Books today.

A copy of the New Testament, printed in Dort, Holland, in 1603, bound in London, c. 1603, in red velvet embroidered with silver thread. The initials ER may mean that the volume was bound for Elizabeth I.
15cm × 10.5cm
Henry Davis Gift

THE MAP LIBRARY

The British Library's collection of maps, both manuscript and printed, is the major cartographic collection in the country, and one of the most important in the world.

The British Museum's foundation collections all included maps. From Sir Robert Cotton's collection came, among other important cartographic items, four 13th-century manuscripts by the St Albans monk, Matthew Paris, in which were included the first scientific maps of Britain to have been produced since the time of Ptolemy (the second century AD). Ptolemy's own *Geographia* in three 15th-century Latin manuscript versions came to the Museum with the Harleian collection. With the old Royal Library, the Museum received such remarkable volumes as the manuscript *Boke of Idrographie* drawn for Henry VIII by Jean Rotz, a former Dieppe pilot, in 1542, and a volume of Christopher Saxton's maps of the counties of England and Wales (1579), many of them extensively annotated by Elizabeth I's minister, Lord Burghley. Among Sir Hans Sloane's collections were many charts and atlases, both manuscript and printed, dating from the 16th and 17th centuries.

George III's library, presented to the Museum in 1828, included superb geographical and topographical materials numbering among its total of some 50,000 maps and charts probably the world's finest collection of maps, plans and charts of 18th-century North America, many of them the results of surveys carried out for military purposes. A map of major political importance in the collection is the 'red-lined map', John Mitchell's map of North America, *c.* 1775, annotated by Richard Oswald, British Commissioner in the negotiations for the Treaty of Paris in 1783. He indicated the demarcation lines between British and French possessions on the continent with a bold red line.

Maritime charts and sea atlases from the King's Library were initially retained by the Admiralty, but were later released to the British Museum and are now in the Map Library. Among them are 17th-century Dutch sea atlases, 18th-century English and French sea atlases and four superb manuscript atlases dated 1682–1700 by William Hack, a hydrographer from Wapping. Hack's 'wagoner of the Great South Sea' – that is, a sea atlas of the Pacific seaboard of America – which was dedicated and presented to Charles II by Capain Bartholomew Sharp, is now one of the treasures of the Map Library. The most remarkable of the atlases presented to Charles II, and now in the Map Library, is the Klencke atlas. This six-feet-high world atlas, containing the finest and largest Dutch maps of the day, was the gift of an Amsterdam merchant, Johan Klencke, to celebrate Charles II's accession and the restoration of the monarchy in 1660.

The founding of the Ordnance Survey in 1791 has provided the

Detail from Ordnance Surveyors' Drawings prepared in 1797 for the first edition 1 inch to 1 mile maps, showing Portsmouth and environs on scale 3 inches to 1 mile.

O.S.D. sh. 75

The Map Library

British Museum and, since 1973, the British Library, with another important source of maps and charts. The Survey's maps have been regularly deposited at Bloomsbury, and the Map Library holds virtually complete sets of all editions of Ordnance survey maps and plans. It also has a number of manuscript maps by 18th-century Ordnance engineers, the forerunners of the Survey proper, which came to the British Museum with George III's Topographical Collection. In addition it holds the Ordnance Survey manuscript drawings prepared between 1790 and 1840 for the first edition one-inch-to-the-mile maps.

Other collections acquired by the British Museum since its foundation and containing much valuable geographical material have included the libraries of Sir Joseph Banks and Thomas Grenville and the Lansdowne manuscripts, all of which were received in the early 19th century. The purchase of the Beudecker Collection in 1861 brought the Museum 24 volumes of maps and views of the Netherlands, 1600–1750, and in 1880 came the Crace Collection of London plans and views. An outstanding recent acquisition was the Royal United Service Institution's sheet map collection which was purchased in 1968.

The right of copyright deposit is another important source of maps, charts and atlases published in Britain, though the right was not fully applied until the 1911 Copyright Act.

From 1844 the map collections of the British Museum were administered as a separate unit, with Richard Henry Major in charge, and between 1867 and 1880 they enjoyed the status of being the Department of Maps and Charts under Major's keepership. From 1882–1892 maps and charts were a sub-department, and in 1892 the manuscript maps (with the exception notably of those in George III's Topographical and Maritime Collection) were transferred to the Department of Manuscripts and the Map Room was established as a section of the Department of Printed Books.

The Department of Manuscripts holds the bulk of the early manuscripts, including much material from the medieval period and numerous charts showing the great European discoveries of the world in the 15th and 16th centuries. Many items, such as Dr John Dee's chart of the northern hemisphere (1580) prepared for Elizabeth I, were made for or used by monarchs. The Map Library basically holds printed maps and charts but there are two major exceptions: the maritime and topographical manuscript maps and charts in the King's Library and the Crace Collection plans are both retained in the Map Library, together with some manuscript maps acquired by it since 1892 which had particular relevance to its collections.

As the British Library is the national repository for British map production, both past and present, so the Map Library is its centre of geographical studies, maintaining a wide-ranging information service and providing reading room facilities, including an open-access reference library, used by several thousand students every year.

Students may call on a collection which contains about two million items, including maps, charts, atlases, globes, and aerial photographs, and which is constantly being added to by purchase, donation, foreign exchange and copyright deposit. About 30,000 sheet maps come into the Map Library every year, most of them continuations of existing series. Good relations with survey departments, production agencies and map producers abroad ensures for the Map Library a steady supply of foreign material, which also comes in under the usual foreign exchange schemes between national libraries.

The main objectives of the Map Library's acquisition policy are to maintain world coverage on topographic scales appropriate to different

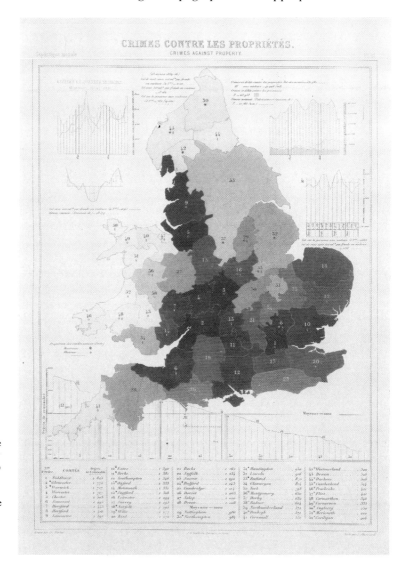

A Map of England and Wales showing crimes against property from the French statistician A. M. Guerry's atlas *Statistique Morale de L'Angleterre comparee avec celle de la France* (1864). Guerry (1802–66) concentrated on investigating the nature of criminality and skilfully converted his findings into statistical maps. He used ten shades from deep brown to white to compare frequency distributions of crime in both France and England.

Maps 32. e. 34.

countries or regions at all periods; to ensure the collection of all important or representative general atlases; and to collect all significant thematic or special-purpose mapping. Not only does the Map Library therefore obtain a wealth of modern map production from all round the world, it also acquires items of historic interest. An important recent acquisition was the *Selenographia*, the earliest English lunar globe, made by John Russell in 1797, and which joined a collection of globes already noteworthy for such items as the earliest known Chinese globe, a terrestrial globe made in China in 1623 by the Jesuit fathers Manuel Dias the younger and Nicolo Longobardi.

Opposite, top left: Detail of the 'red-line map' made by John Mitchell *c.* 1775, and annotated to show the boundary of the new republic of the United States of America by Richard Oswald, 1782–3

K. Top. CXVII. 49b

Bottom left: Danish official survey maps are produced by the Geodaetisk Institut. This is a section of sheet 1513-IV-SQ: Roskilde (1975) from their series *Danmark* *1 : 25,000*.

34420. (82.)

Top right: This map of the area around the Susten Pass in the Swiss Alps is from sheet 255: Sustenpass (1976) of the national series *Landeskarte der Schweiz* *1 : 50,000* published by the Bundesamt für Landestopographie.

24405. (131.)

Bottom right: The series *Tactical pilotage chart* is the military version of the aeronautical chart covering most of the world at a scale of 1 : 500,000. Seen here is a section of sheet G-3A (1980) showing Athens and Euboea.

921. (19*.)

A terrestrial globe made in China in AD 1623. The globe, painted in lacquer on wood 58 cm in diameter, is made on a scale 1 : 21,000,000.

Maps C. 6. a. 2.

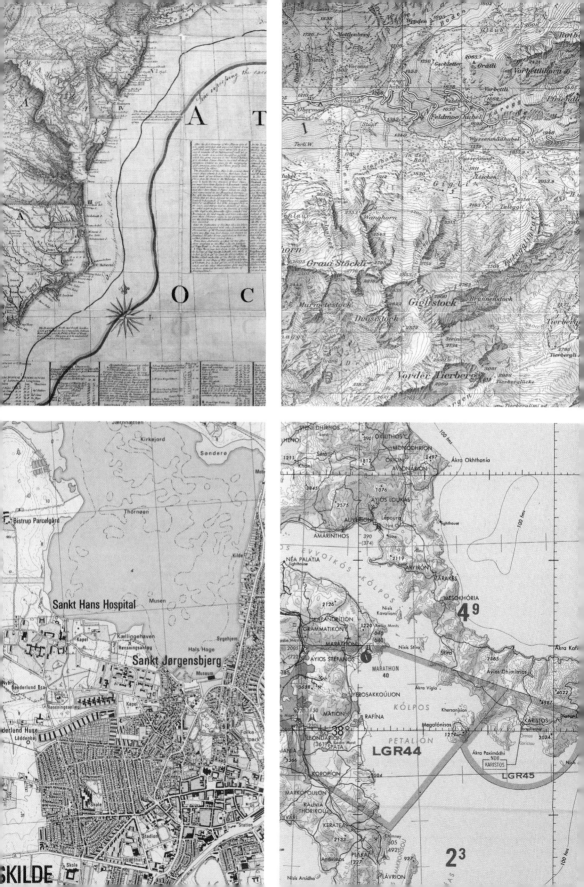

RURAL BEAUTY, or VAUXHAL GARDEN.

THE MUSIC LIBRARY

The Music Library, a branch of the Department of Printed Books, is the British Library's repository for printed music scores. As with other departments of the Reference Division, so one may say of the Music Library that its holdings are incomparably the finest in the United Kingdom, while very few other libraries elsewhere in the world can rival its remarkable breadth of representation of all periods, types of musical publication and countries of origin.

The collection of more than one and a quarter million pieces of music covers the history of printed music from its beginnings in the 16th century to the present day and ranges from lute tablatures, 16th-century part books, song books, chamber and orchestral music including many important early editions of the great composers and the full scores of 19th-century operas to the most recent scores in new types of musical notation.

Books about music, including history, theory and biography, are not kept in the Music Library but in the General Library. This does not affect the reader, however, as music and books alike can be consulted together in the Music Reading Area. Musical theory in oriental languages will be found in the Department of Oriental Manuscripts and Printed Books.

As it is the national music library, the Music Library aims to be as complete an archive as possible of every aspect of British musical publication, without exception. Although much of its modern British music comes to it as a result of copyright deposit requirements, these have been frequently disregarded, at least until early this century, and the Library does not claim to hold every piece of music, popular or otherwise, published in Britain. Filling the gaps remains an important part of the Music Library's acquisitions policy.

In the 18th and early 19th centuries, the British Museum authorities regarded printed sheet music as of lesser importance than the printed word and also difficult to catalogue or shelve, so that it was not until the 1840s that it was properly bound and catalogued and any serious collecting attempted. However, in the second half of the 19th century, the Museum acquired great quantities of antiquarian music from all countries which laid the foundation of the present collections.

While the Music Library has a never-ending task in ensuring as complete a coverage as possible of British music, it must be more selective in the contents of its international collection. The Library purchases new publications from every continent and can show a wide spectrum of the work of contemporary composers published abroad as well as all standard scholarly editions of old music. It does not collect foreign popular music, considering this to be the responsibility of the various national libraries concerned, but is constantly expanding its

Plate 21 from Vol. 1 of
The Musical Entertainer
by George Bickham,
London 1737. This is a
song for Vauxhall Gardens
by William Boyce, with an
appropriate illustration.
Music Library.

K. 10. b. 12.

33

holdings in foreign antiquarian music of every kind.

While the Department of Manuscripts is the British Library's home for most manuscript music, the Music Library also has substantial holdings of music manuscripts among the printed works. This is because it is the repository of two outstanding music libraries which came into the British Museum in this century.

The first was the Royal Music Library, deposited on loan by George V in 1911, and presented to the British Museum by Elizabeth II in 1957 in commemoration of the donation to the Museum of the old Royal Library by George II two hundred years before. Because the Royal Music Library is an historic entity, its contents have not been split up, but are retained in their entirety in the Music Library.

The foundations of the Royal Music Library were laid in the 18th century, largely in the reign of George III, although a nucleus had been brought over from Hanover. George III and Queen Charlotte were genuine music lovers, and their music librarians evidently had licence to collect not only material for practical use but items of antiquarian interest as well. A considerable part of the Royal Music Library consisted of manuscripts, and included autograph scores of Purcell, Alessandro Scarlatti, Handel and J. C. Bach. The Handel autograph series is particularly splendid, filling 97 volumes, and is augmented by many contemporary copies and early printed editions of his work. The Royal Library also has earlier manuscript music, notably the Forster and Cosyn virginal books and a collection of motets, madrigals and other music compiled by John Baldwin. Under Queen Victoria much 19th-century printed music was added to the Royal Library.

The second great acquisition of this century was the Hirsch Library of nearly 20,000 volumes of printed music and music literature, and some manuscript material, ranging from the 15th century to the present. Paul Hirsch was a Frankfurt businessman who began collecting music while in his teens. Forced to leave Germany in the 1930s, he came to Britain, bringing his music collection with him. In 1946 he sold it to the British Museum, generously accepting a lower sum than he might have received from the United States so that his tremendous library might remain in Britain.

Paul Hirsch was particularly interested in early theory and in first and early editions of the Viennese classics, a field in which the Music Library had previously been somewhat deficient. The acquisition of the Hirsch Library, plus the earlier purchase of duplicates from the Gesellschaft der Musikfreunde in Vienna, thus brought this particular section of the Library's holdings up to strength.

Visitors to the British Library will find in the King's Library a permanent exhibition of items from the Music Library's collections illustrating the history of music printing. Examples of the four processes – wood or metal block, metal type, engraved plates and lithography – by which music has been printed since the early 16th century, are on show.

The autograph manuscript of the Quartet in C Major ('The Dissonance': K465) by Wolfgang Amadeus Mozart, completed in January 1785.
22·5cm × 32cm.
Add. MS 37763, f. 57

George Frederick Handel's autograph manuscript of the *Music for the Royal Fireworks*, 1749, in the Music Library collection. This illustration shows the movement entitled 'La Rejouissance.'
R. M. 20. g. 7.

Those who wish to study the Music Library's collections in depth should obtain a reader's ticket to allow them access to the Music Reading Area in the Official Publications Library.

Opposite: A page from Peter Maxwell Davies's *Eight songs for a mad king*, reproduced from the composer's autograph manuscript, London 1971. The notation represents the bird cage in which George III kept the bullfinches which he tried to teach to sing, and perhaps also the cage in which his own madness imprisoned him. Music Library. (By permission of Boosey and Hawkes Music Publishers Ltd.)
I. 525. 55.

Below left: The title page of Sir William Leighton's *The Teares or Lamentacions of a sorrowfull soule*, London 1614. This copy was owned by Prince Charles, later King Charles I, to whom the work was dedicated. Leighton persuaded nearly every English composer of note to contribute settings of his poems to the collection. Music Library.
K. 1. i. 9.

Below right: The title page of *The Railway Foot Warmer* by Charles D'Ace, 1880, in the Music Library. The significance of the horrified aesthete seen through the window in this Victorian illustration is unclear.
H. 1787. e. (25)

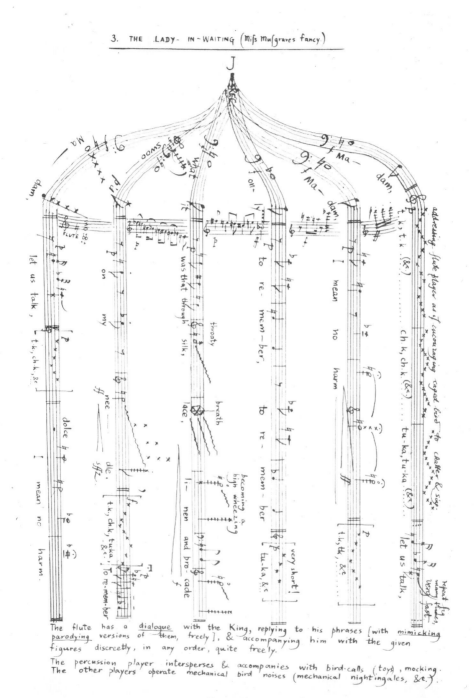

3. THE LADY-IN-WAITING (Miss Musgraves fancy.)

The flute has a dialogue with the King, replying to his phrases [with mimicking parodying versions of them, freely], & accompanying him with the given figures discreetly, in any order, quite freely.

The percussion player intersperses & accompanies with bird-calls (toys), mocking. The other players operate mechanical bird noises (mechanical nightingales, &c.).

12

37

*William Nixon, High Street,
Stony Stratford*

THE COTTAGE NEWSPAPER.

And General Advertiser for Stony Stratford and surrounding District.

No. 618]   STONY STRATFORD; JANUARY 25, 1867.   [PRICE 1D.

THE NEWSPAPER LIBRARY

The United Kingdom's national collection of newspapers is held by the British Library in the Newspaper Library, a branch of the Department of Printed Books, at Colindale in north London. The Newspaper Library holds well over half a million volumes and parcels of newspapers, including both national and provincial British daily and weekly newspapers, as well as some journals and periodicals and large collections of Commonwealth and foreign newspapers. Parts of the collection are kept in central London. Newspapers published in London before 1801 are in the main library in Great Russell Street and newspapers in oriental languages are held by the Department of Oriental Manuscripts and Printed Books and the India Office Library and Records.

Although there were a few newspapers among Sir Hans Sloane's books, the founding of the British Library's newspaper collection really dates from 1762, when George III bought and presented to the British Museum the large collection of tracts made during the English Civil War and Commonwealth period by a London bookseller, George Thomason, of the Rose and Crown in St Paul's Churchyard.

Thomason believed that the tracts, pamphlets, journals and other ephemera printed in Britain and Europe in the years of turmoil after 1640 would be of considerable interest in the future, and he collected omnivorously up to and for a time after the coronation of Charles II in 1661. The 'Thomason Tracts' numbered over 22,000 items, of which more than 7,000 were numbers or editions of newspapers.

The Burney Collection, purchased by the Museum in 1818, brought it many newspapers. Nearly all the British Library's very early British newspapers came to it in the Burney Collection, beginning with *News from Holland* (1619) and including others printed before 1640. The Burney Collection was also rich in 18th-century newspapers, including Scottish newspapers from 1708, English provincial newspapers from 1712, and many American newspapers.

The British Museum did not begin receiving newspapers under the Copyright Acts until 1869. Before this, it acquired its newspapers mainly through the Stamp Office, which collected and held newspapers under the terms of various Stamp Acts. The Stamp Office began regularly sending those London newspapers which it had held for three years to the Museum in 1823; provincial newspapers came in from 1832 and Scottish and Irish papers from 1848.

The Cottage Newspaper, an interesting example of a mid-19th century English provincial newspaper in the Newspaper Library collection. The advertisements reflect the rural nature of the paper's circulation area.
51cm × 36cm

Always difficult objects to store because of their size and bulk or to make available to readers because of their essential fragility, the newspaper collection posed something of a problem for the Museum until, in 1902, it began storing them away from the Bloomsbury site, at Hendon.

The Hendon site, or Colindale, as it is now called, grew from being simply a repository for lesser used newspapers into a fully-fledged

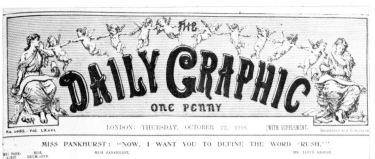

The immediacy of the moment is conveyed by this illustration from The Daily Graphic, 1908, in the Newspaper Library. 42cm × 30cm

Newspaper Library, complete with Reading Room and ancillary services. Despite the loss of 10,000 volumes and the damaging of a further 20,000 volumes when the Colindale storage block was bombed during World War II, the Library's collections today are extensive and are constantly augmented by donations, purchase and copyright deposit.

Acquisitions are not necessarily of whole newspapers or journals: the *Daily Express* newspaper in London recently donated to the Newspaper Library a collection of more than one million biographical press clippings covering some 36,700 individuals. Once sorted and microfilmed, the collection will provide a previously untapped source of information for users.

While acquiring newspapers and journals from all parts of the world and making them available to readers remains the Newspaper Library's primary function, it also plays an important role as a central source of information for other newspaper libraries and archives. For example, the Library is at present forming a union list of newspaper indexes and clipping files in local library systems throughout the country which will provide an invaluable research aid for students and scholars.

The wear and tear to which newspapers are subjected in use is a continuing problem. Once, the main method of conservation was to ensure that the newspapers were all well bound and stored. Today's alternative answer, and one which is being used by libraries in all parts of the world, is to put newspapers on microfilm, thus ensuring the survival of the originals for the future.

The Newspaper Library's microfilm programme, which includes both purchases and its own films, has already made available to readers more than 150,000 microfilm reels of newspapers, ranging from the mere 14 feet (very imperfect) of the *Flying Post*, or *Post-Master* published in Dublin between 1708 and 1710, to the 514 reels of the *Evening Standard*, 1860–1968. Five hundred volumes of British national newspapers are available to readers only on microfilm.

The Library's microfilm programme also means that copies of runs of newspapers can be provided for other libraries and archives.

The ingenuity of The Mafeking Mail's publishers was tried to its limits during the Boer War seige of the town between 1 November 1899 and 15 June 1900. Towards the end, the 'Seige slip' was printed on any materials which were to hand, including accounts paper and brown wrapping paper. Newspaper Library. 38cm × 25cm

THE MAFEKING MAIL
SPECIAL SEIGE SLIP.

ISSUED DAILY, SHELLS PERMITTING.   ONLY TERMS: ONE SHILLING PER WEEK, PAYABLE IN ADVANCE.

No. 1   **Mafeking, November 1st, 1899.**

Technical difficulties prevented the issue of the "Mafeking Mail" for Saturday last. Those difficulties we hope speedily to surmount. In the meantime we purpose keeping our friends informed of, happenings from day to day; "Oud Kraker" or "Black Maria" *et hoc genus omne* permitting

The Mafeking Mail.

MAFEKING, 1st NOVEMBER, 1899.

tional circumstances thrust upon us could have made possible, we are in a position to judge and recognise the steady determination that British blood and British pluck exhibit when such a crisis as the present arises, and we know that the memory of Bronkhurst Spruit, Majuba and Potchefstrom will make that determination, supported by the knowledge of our grand successes of the past fortnight more firm, more strong and more united than has been before, and this, with the grand soldier, who is in command here, will render certain the first stages towards

Boer's fitness to dominate such a territory as the Transvaal. Let it be placed, say, in the space opposite the entrance to the Railway Station, raised on end, with the unexploded shells piled at its base, with a description of Colonel Baden-Powell's clever defence of the place. We hope the Colonel will bear the town in mind when the disposal of the gun is under discussion.

Major Lord E. Cecil, C.S.O., last evening issued the following under the heading of General

THE OFFICIAL PUBLICATIONS
LIBRARY

This Library, situated near the British Museum's north entrance in Montague Place, is the reading room for the Department of Printed Books' holdings of British and foreign official publications, an enormous collection and the principal one of its kind in the country.

The basis of the service is the official papers published by the state in this country over several centuries. Parliamentary Commons papers, the Journals and Debates of both Houses of Parliament, and Acts of Parliament, are on open shelves and latest issues of Command papers, Bills, Debates, Acts and press releases are generally on the Official Publications Library open access shelves within a day of receipt. There are also the census reports, and current United Kingdom electoral registers.

Readers will also find on the open access shelves the reference collection for the social sciences. Guides to subject areas, indexing and abstracting journals, published catalogues of other libraries and other bibliographic aids provide general help in such subjects as sociology, demography, social and economic geography, anthropology, education, economics and law. Reference works for the social sciences are arranged by the Dewey Decimal classification with which most library users are familiar.

There are also the current issues of the *Economist, New Scientist, New Society, The Times Educational Supplement* and *The Times Higher Educational Supplement, The Times, Financial Times, Le Monde* and the *International Herald Tribune*.

While the material on open access is generally that most often called upon by readers, it represents only a tiny fraction of the library's total collections of official papers; two large storehouses in Woolwich are required to hold the bulk of the collection.

The historical collections are of world-wide importance. The Department of Printed Books began seriously to build up its collections of official papers and publications in the mid-19th century and in stages since the 1880s has established a system of international exchange which brings in a wealth of government-published material from all over the world. Governments of the former colonies of the Empire were a rich source of material as a result of a Colonial Office instruction that the Museum Library must be sent all official books, documents and maps, however trivial they might seem, an instruction for which countless scholars and students of British colonial and imperial history and, indeed, of the histories of the former colonies themselves, have had cause to be grateful. Material survives – not only from the former colonies – which has not survived in the country of origin, and large microfilm orders from overseas are frequently supplied.

The variety of material and the variety of its subject-content are greater than might be believed from the rather dry term, 'official publications'. The collections include the first published surveys of large parts of the world, the great 19th-century studies of social conditions, recipe books and manuals of nutrition from developing countries, and the transcripts of the Watergate tapes, to name only a few examples.

The Library's emphasis is not only on the historical collections, but also on the provision of current information, particularly in the areas of government policy-making, statistics, and overseas law where it forms part of the British Library's Business Information Service, and there are information services for readers on the spot, computer search services, and telephone enquiry services for outside users.

(R) AS 187/189(2)

[2nd copy]

Submission of

Recorded Presidential Conversations

To the

Committee on the Judiciary

of the

House of Representatives

by

President Richard Nixon

April 30, 1974

One of the Official Publications Library's copies of the transcript of the Watergate Tapes. Washington 1974

(R) AS 187/182 (2)

THE PHILATELIC COLLECTION

The British Library's Philatelic Collection is very broadly based with an international coverage, taking in revenue material and fiscal stamps as well as postage stamps. It also contains much ephemera such as propaganda labels, exhibition vignettes and labels, and new issue publicity hand-outs, which provide invaluable information on production, printing and the artists who produced the original designs, as well as more closely related material such as postal stationery, and telegraph, customs and other stamped forms.

The collections, which today number approximately 6 million items and contain over 30 identifiable collections and archives, began with the bequeathing to the British Museum of the Tapling Collection in 1891. This vast collection, made by Thomas Keay Tapling, M.P., fell into two parts: postage stamps, of which there were some 50,000; and postal stationery, including postcards, lettercards, stamped envelopes, registered mail, telegraph and customs forms and many other items. The coverage of both parts is world-wide and extends to proofs, varieties and errors. It also includes many unique items. Examples of the famous and now very rare Mauritius one penny and twopenny stamps, which the engraver inscribed 'Post Office' instead of 'Post Paid', are in the Tapling Collection.

Although Thomas Tapling's bequest may be said to be the foundation stone of the British Library's Philatelic Collection, its main postage stamp reference collection today is the Universal Postal Union collection, which currently increases by some 12,000 items annually. These come, via the British Post Office, from the Universal Postal Union in Berne, Switzerland, which distributes among its members reference sets of every new postage stamp issued by members, who now include virtually all the postal administrations of the world.

Another collection in the British Library's care is that of the Crown Agents, who supply the Library with sets of all the stamps they produce for their clients. The Library also holds the Crown Agents' modern archive, dating in the main from the 1950s, which contains many examples of artists' preliminary sketches, final artwork and proofs for stamps.

The Philatelic Collection has three large air mail collections in which may be found many items of considerable historic interest. The Fitzgerald Collection, for instance, has several items connected with Alcock and Brown's first non-stop transatlantic flight, including the $1 payment cheque for the carriage of the first air mail bag. There is also a piece of the fabric from the plane in which Alcock crashed and was killed in France in 1919. A letter written by the R100's constructor, Sir Deniston Burney, on the airship's printed stationery during the flight to Canada describes the flight, and the food and accommodation on

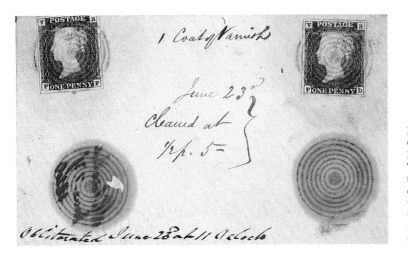

Historic stamps from Great Britain in the Philatelic Section's Tapling Collection: two of the 'VR' 1d blacks used for obliteration tests. These were intended for official use, but were never issued. The handwriting is that of Rowland Hill.

board, and speculates on the future speed of international travel.

The Fitzgerald Collection, assembled by an American, Augustine Fitzgerald, is international in its coverage, though the volume for Great Britain was lost when Mrs Fitzgerald had to flee France ahead of the German advance in 1940. The gap was more than well covered by the donation to the British Library of the H. Eric Scott Collection, which covers all aspects of the development of the air post service in Great Britain, including the carriage of mail by helicopter and hovercraft.

One of the Philatelic Collection's main fiscal collections is the massive Board of Inland Revenue Stamp Archive, deposited with the British Museum in 1966. This dates back to 1710, when the Stamping Office appears to have begun keeping proper records of stamps printed, though the Philatelic Collection includes a specialised collection of revenue stamps from the early days of the Stamping Office, 1694–1710. The range of the Inland Revenue Archive is very wide and covers stamps both for taxes imposed and taxes proposed but not implemented. An example of the latter in the Archive is a 19th-century tax on matches for which the stamp was produced and printed but never used as the tax was not imposed. The similar fate of a tax on luxuries proposed at the time of the First World War may also be traced in the Inland Revenue Archive.

The British Library does not buy items for its Philatelic Collection, everything in it having come as a gift, donation, bequest or other, similar form of acquisition. Although only a tiny fraction of the Philatelic Collection is on display in the King's Library, the Collection is available to visitors by appointment.

THE READING ROOM

The fame of the British Library's Reading Room rests partly on its design, which is an impressive example of Victorian architectural and building skills. Constructed basically of cast iron, and open to readers in 1857, just eight years after it was first conceived, its outstanding feature is the 106-foot-high dome, whose 140-foot diameter is only two feet less than that of the Pantheon in Rome and is greater than the domes of both St Peter's in Rome and St Paul's in the City of London.

The dome's ribs are supported on 20 cast-iron piers enclosed by brick. Between them, tall arched windows reach up 27 feet from the top of the three levels of bookshelves which line the walls.

Thirty thousand reference books are available on open access in the Reading Room, including dictionaries, indexes, bibliographic catalogues, encyclopedias and other works arranged in subject categories. In the centre of the room is the general library catalogue and the catalogues of maps and newspapers. Elsewhere in the room is a growing catalogue on microfiches of books received in recent years. The collections are kept in stacks, originally also constructed of cast iron as a fire precaution, built round the Reading Room and in various other rooms and stores, some several miles from the Bloomsbury building. Books are delivered to readers on application.

The collections are, of course, the main reason for the fame of the Reading Room. Their wide-ranging richness, which permits scholars to work in many disciplines, has attracted readers as diverse in their interests and influences as Karl Marx, Lenin and Gandhi, Disraeli and Gladstone, Dickens and G.B. Shaw. The latter was so grateful for the study facilities available to him in the Reading Room that he bequeathed a large part of his estate to the British Museum; both Museum and Library have benefited, in particular from the success of *Pygmalion's* musical version, *My Fair Lady*.

The Reading Room is on view to visitors every hour on the hour from 11.00–16.00, Monday–Friday.

Opposite: 'The Nativity' from the Benedictional of St Ethelwold, made *c.* AD 980 for St Ethelwold, Bishop of Winchester 963–84, by a monk named Godeman. It is the outstanding example of the so-called 'Winchester School' of illumination, which flourished in England in the century preceding the Norman conquest. 29.5cm × 22cm

Add. MS 49598, f. 15b

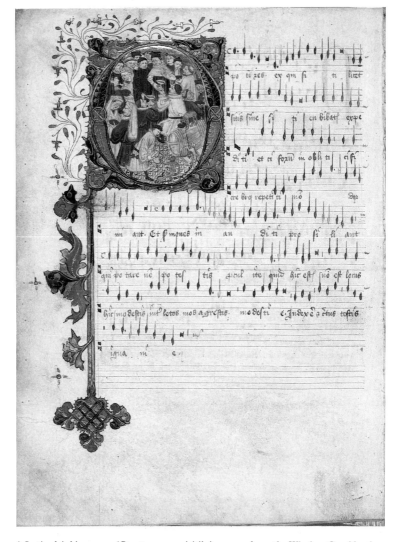

A Latin drinking song, 'O potores exquisiti', in a page from the Windsor Carol book. The manuscript was probably made between 1430 and 1444 for St George's Chapel at Windsor Castle.

Egerton MS 3307, f.72b

Overleaf: The opening of St Luke's Gospel from the Lindisfarne Gospels, the famous manuscript of the Four Gospels which is one of the first and greatest masterpieces of medieval European book illumination. It was made *c.* AD 698 in the Northumbrian island monastery of Lindisfarne, probably to mark the translation of the relics of St Cuthbert. The scribe and illuminator, a monk named Eadfrith, afterwards became Bishop of Lindisfarne. 34cm × 25cm

Cotton Ms. Nero D iv, f. 139

✠ lucas ualus ꝃ
on gyned   god ꝛpoll   epɩ   lucuɣ
ɪɴcɪpɪꞇ euanꞇelium   secuꞇ duu lucam ··
                                        fron ƿor

QUO
NIAM
          ꝵec   fod
QUIDE
          monɩʒo   cunnendo
MULTIcoNAM
          poꞇꝛon   þꞇe luɩ ʒꞇ
TISUNꞇORDINA
en ꝺe bꝛodnuꝺ on   ꝺuꞇ ʒꞇaʒa
RENARRATIONEM

are ferrets! Where <u>can</u> I have dropped them,
I wonder?" Alice guessed in a moment that
it was looking for the nosegay and the pair
of white kid gloves, and she began hunting
for them, but they were now nowhere to be
seen — everything seemed to have changed
since her swim in the pool, and her walk
along the river—bank with its fringe of
rushes and forget—me—nots, and the glass
table and the little door had vanished.

Soon the rabbit
noticed Alice, as
she stood looking
curiously about
her, and at once
said in a quick
angry tone, "why,
Mary Ann! what
<u>are</u> you doing out
here? Go home this
moment, and look

on my dressing-table for my gloves and nosegay,
and fetch them here, as quick as you can
run, do you hear?" and Alice was so much
frightened that she ran off at once, without

DEPARTMENT
OF MANUSCRIPTS

A page from the autograph manuscript of Lewis Carroll's *Alice's Adventures Under Ground*, written and illustrated by the author between July 1862 and February 1863 for Alice Liddell, daughter of the Dean of Christ Church, Oxford. The book was subsequently expanded to nearly twice the length and published in 1865 as *Alice's Adventures in Wonderland*.
18.5cm × 11.7cm
Add. MS 46700, f. 45b

The Department of Manuscripts was, as we have seen, one of the three original departments of the British Museum, along with the Department of Printed Books and the Department of Natural and Artificial Productions. When the Museum was opened in 1759, the manuscripts in its collections came from the Cotton, Harley, Sloane and old Royal libraries. How these libraries came to form the foundation of the British Museum has already been described. The manuscripts thus brought together were a magnificent collection in themselves; today, after two centuries of further acquisitions, the Department possesses one of the largest and finest collections in the world, containing manuscripts of all kinds and all ages in Western languages: Greek and Latin papyri, ancient Biblical codices, illuminated manuscripts of incalculable value, other medieval manuscripts both secular and religious, great archives of post-medieval historical papers, famous literary autographs, and vast collections of music, maps, plans, topographical drawings, charters and seals.

Manuscripts belonging to particular named collections are numbered within that collection. In most cases the numbering is straight through; for example, the Harley collection is numbered from 1 to 7660; on the other hand the Cotton and Royal collections have retained earlier press-marks. Sir Robert Cotton's library was a narrow room with fourteen presses, each one surmounted by the bust of one of the twelve Roman Caesars together with the two imperial ladies, Cleopatra and Faustina. Thus Cotton MS Nero D iv (the *Lindisfarne Gospels*) was originally the fourth manuscript along on the fourth shelf down (shelf D) in the press with the bust of Nero on top. In the case of the old Royal Library the presses were numbered rather than named (e.g. Royal MS 20 C iii).

The Sloane manuscripts on the other hand were numbered from 1 to 4100 after their reception in the British Museum. It is this collection which is considered to be the true basis of the Department's holdings; most of the manuscripts which have been acquired since 1756 have been numbered in a series of 'Additional' manuscripts which started from 4101 and had reached 62,000 by 1982. However a few large collections were acquired in their entirety and have retained their own

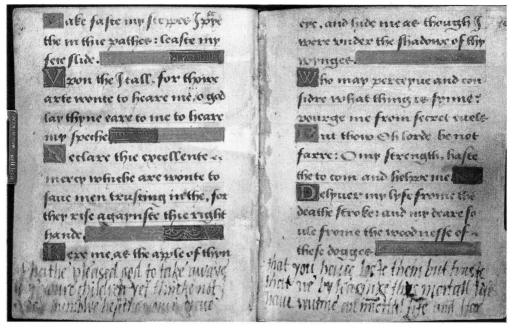

This small Manual of Prayers, in actuality almost the same size as it is here reproduced, is believed to have been used by Lady Jane Grey on the scaffold, 12 February 1554. The note in her hand at the foot of the pages is addressed to her father, the Duke of Suffolk. 9.5cm × 7.5cm

Harley MS 2342, ff. 78b–79

This harvest scene is a marginal decoration from the Luttrell Psalter, a Latin manuscript celebrated for its long series of marginal illustrations showing lively scenes of daily life in medieval England. The Psalter was written and illuminated *c.* 1335–40 for Sir Geoffrey Luttrell of Irnham in Lincolnshire. 35cm × 24.5cm

Add. MS 42130, f. 173b (detail)

Above: The Expedition of the Duc de
Bourbon to Barbary, from Froissart's
Chronicle. This miniature is in a late 15th-
century manuscript of Jean Froissart's
Chroniques de France et d'Angleterre,
executed in Paris for the French historian
Philip de Commines (d. 1509). 42cm × 31cm

Harley MS 4379, f. 60b

Right: Detail from a calendar page showing
the occupation of the month and sign of the
Zodiac for the month of August, from the
Bedford Hours. This Book of Hours was
written and illuminated in Paris for John,
Duke of Bedford, brother of Henry V, and
Regent of France, *c.* 1423. 26cm × 18cm

Add. MS 18850, f. 8

separate numeration. The number of a manuscript appears in the descriptive label of each item on exhibition.

Individual manuscript items may be anything from a single document to a book containing as many as 500 or more leaves. The Department usually binds groups of single documents, such as letters, into volumes for ease of handling; the main part of the collection now comprises upwards of 100,000 such volumes. The visitor to the Library's galleries may see a considerable number of them stored in the glass-fronted presses in the Manuscript Saloon.

The breadth of the collection is enormous and it is impossible to do more than outline briefly what is contained in it. The permanent exhibition attempts to give a reasonably comprehensive impression but even this is the merest tip of the iceberg.

The term 'manuscript' for many people means a medieval manuscript and the Department certainly has a collection in this field unparalleled in this country. The series of English and continental illuminated manuscripts displayed in the Grenville Library gives some idea, not only of the richness of the collection, but also of the history of medieval art, for it is mainly in the illuminated manuscript that the painting of the period has survived. The Library's greatest artistic treasure is perhaps the *Lindisfarne Gospels*, a copy of the four gospels which was written and illuminated in the monastery of Lindisfarne, on Holy Island, about AD 698; the *Harley Golden Gospels* dates from a century later; it was made about AD 800 at the court of Charlemagne; the *Benedictional of St Ethelwold* (963–984), a collection of pontifical blessings for use at mass on different days of the year, is the finest surviving example of Anglo-Saxon art of the Winchester School. Other notable illuminated manuscripts are *Queen Mary's Psalter* and the *Luttrell Psalter*, both produced in England during the first half of the 14th century, and the *Bedford Hours*, a masterpiece of French book painting of the early 15th century.

Of enormous importance are the two great early manuscripts of the Bible, the *Codex Sinaiticus* of the mid–4th century and the *Codex Alexandrinus* of the early 5th century. There are many important medieval literary manuscripts: two examples are the manuscripts in the Cotton collection which are the unique sources of *Beowulf*, the oldest epic in English (*c.* 1000), and of *Sir Gawain and the Green Knight* (late 14th century).

Thousands of legal documents of various kinds, many from the medieval period, are preserved in the Department: the most famous are two of the four surviving examples of the earliest issue of *Magna Carta*. Unfortunately one of the two was badly damaged in a fire which occurred in the Cotton Library in 1731 and is now virtually illegible. The two are exhibited together with other related documents in a special case in the Manuscript Saloon.

One important area in which the collections are rich is that of historical papers: the letters and other papers of statesmen, ministers, diplomats etc. Some survive from medieval times, but the collection comes into its own in the Tudor period, since when every stage of British history is well represented. The papers of Lord Burghley, the Tudor statesman, and of the first Duke of Marlborough (known as the Blenheim Papers, a recent acquisition) are just two examples of the many collections that are to be found. Nineteenth-century politicians are especially well represented; the collections of W. E. Gladstone are so extensive that a complete volume of the catalogue is devoted to them.

The cases of literary autographs in the permanent exhibition will give some idea of the breadth of coverage in this field: most of the important figures of English literature are represented either by manuscripts of works or by letters. Although clearly smaller in scope, the Department's holdings also include a significant number of manuscripts of foreign writers.

An important collection of manuscript maps reflects the gradual exploration of the world, although alongside world atlases may be found local estate maps of every period. In another field, that of music, the Department has a collection which is not only unrivalled as a source for the history of English music but also contains autographs of many of the great composers – Bach, Handel, Haydn, Mozart, Beethoven, Schubert and so on. Particular attention has been paid to building up collections of the manuscripts of modern British composers such as Elgar, Vaughan Williams, Holst, Britten and Tippett.

Finally some special categories of manuscripts must be mentioned: Greek and Latin papyri (mostly recovered from excavations in Egypt); Greek *ostraca* (potsherds with writing); seals; and playscripts (the plays submitted to the Lord Chamberlain from 1824 to 1968 have been transferred to the British Library and the collection is still being added to as theatre managements are required by law to provide a copy of any new play performed in public).

As has been said, only a minute proportion of the Department's collection can be put on general exhibition. A reading room in the Department is equipped to enable those who need to have access to items in the collection to do so. It holds about 60 readers and has a small specialist reference library.

As the Department of Printed Books is the national repository of the printed word in all its forms, so is the Department of Manuscripts the national repository of the written word. Written documents have an immediacy that no printed document can achieve; we are brought into direct contact with the past when we see, for example, a letter written by Princess Elizabeth to her half-brother Edward VI. The visitor who spends an hour or two in the manuscripts exhibition will find himself immersed in the history of Western civilisation in general and of this country in particular.

Like, as a shipman in stormy wether plukes downe the sailes taryng(e)
for bettar winde, so did I, most noble Kinge, in my vnfortu(nat)
chanche a thurday pluk(ed) downe the hie sailes of my ioy, (and) ca(re)
and do trust one day that as troblesome wanes haue repu(lsed)
me bakwarde, so a gentil winde wil bringe me forwarde (to)
my hauen. Two chief occasions moued me muche and
grined me gretly, the one for that I douted your Maies(ties)
helthe, the other bicause for al my longe taryinge I wen(t)
without that I came for, of the first I am ~~wel~~ releued i(n)
a parte, bothe that I vnderstode of your helthe and al(so)
that your Maiesties logginge is far fro my Lorde Marqu(es)
chamber, Of my other grief I am not eased, but the b(est)
is that whatsoeuer other folkes wil suspect, I intende no(t)
to feare your graces goodwil, wiche as I knowe that (I)
I neuer disarued to faint, so I trust wil stil stike by m(e)
For if your graces admis that I shulde retourne (wh(ose)
wil is a comandemente) had not bine, I wold not haue (
made the halfe of my way, the ende of my iourney.
And thus as one desirous to hire of your Maiesties hel(the)
thogth vnfortunat to se it I shal pray God for euer (to)
preserue you. From Hatfilde this present saterday

Your Maiesties huble (sister)
to comandemente Elisabeth

A letter written by Queen Elizabeth I, when Princess Elizabeth, to her half-brother, Edward VI. Much of the atmosphere of suspicion and danger which surrounded Elizabeth during her early years is revealed in this letter. It is clear that Elizabeth has attempted to see her brother, perhaps during his final illness in 1553, but has been turned away.
30cm × 19.4cm
Harley MS 6986, f.23

The House of Commons, as shown on the reverse of the 'Great Seal of England 1651', the second seal used by the Commonwealth. The scene shows the House in session, with the Speaker in the chair, a member addressing the House, and two Clerks at the table upon which the mace is laid. Diameter: 14.5cm

Seal xxxiv. 17.

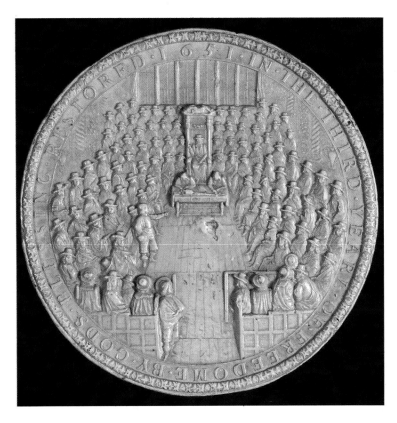

Nelson's last letter, written to Lady Hamilton on board the *Victory*, 19 October 1805. A postscript dated 20 October, the eve of the Battle of Trafalgar, gives details of the enemy fleet as it drew up. Emma Hamilton has added at the end: 'This letter was found open on *His* Desk & brought to Lady Hamilton by Cap^n Hardy. Oh miserable wretched Emma oh glorious & happy Nelson.' 24cm × 18.5cm

Egerton MS 1614, ff. 125b–126

凡欲讀經先念淨口業真言三遍

循唎　循唎

摩訶循唎

循循唎

婆婆訶

奉請除穢金剛

奉請辟妖金剛

奉請黃隨求金剛

DEPARTMENT OF ORIENTAL MANUSCRIPTS AND PRINTED BOOKS

The frontispiece from the Diamond Sutra, the world's earliest dated printed book. Found in a walled-up cave library at Dunhuang in 1907 by the archaeologist Sir Marc Aurel Stein, it is printed from a series of wooden blocks, and carries a date equivalent to AD 11 May 868. The standard of craftsmanship in the cutting of the frontispiece, which shows the Buddha preaching to his aged disciple Subhuti, may be taken as evidence for a substantial body of experience in the art of printing prior to the 9th century. The text of the Diamond Sutra is the Chinese version of the Sanskrit Vajraccedikā-prajñāpāramita-sūtra. Frontispiece: 23.9cm × 28.6cm
Or. 8210/P.2.

The British Library's oriental-language collections, apart from books on modern science and technology in oriental languages which are held in the Science Reference Library, total over half a million books, 40,000 manuscripts, and other items, and are in the care of the Department of Oriental Manuscripts and Printed Books.

Among the many treasures which help to make these collections some of the finest in the world, as well as the largest in the United Kingdom, are the collection of Chinese oracle bones dating back to the Shang period of the second millennium BC, which constitute a substantial part of the evidence for the earliest forms of Chinese characters; the set of eight Buddhist charms (*Hyakumanto-dharani*) from Japan which are the world's earliest printed texts datable with some certainty, as they were issued by the Empress Shōtoku, who reigned AD 764 to 770; and the *Diamond Sutra* found at Dunhuang in China, the world's earliest known dated printed document, bearing a year date equivalent to AD 868.

The British Museum's foundation collections contained an appreciable amount of oriental material, including Anglo-Jewish charters and Hebrew, Arabic and Turkish manuscripts in the Harleian collection, and Hebrew, Sanskrit and Tamil manuscripts in the Sloane collection, with other materials coming in from later collections. The Museum's oriental holdings began to increase rapidly in the 19th century, when many oriental items and whole collections, acquired by British explorers, travellers, colonial administrators and diplomats, came to the British Museum.

Claudius Rich, for example, whose very fine collections of antiquities and Near Eastern manuscripts were bought by Parliament for the British Museum in 1825, was British Resident in Baghdad. His son-in-law, William Erskine, was an expert on Indian history and his papers, including examples of Jain literature and Hindi and Punjabi religious poems as well as historical texts, were presented to the Museum in 1865. Sir Henry Rawlinson, an archaeologist who was also British

Rama and his monkey allies storming the stronghold of Ravana: an illustration, painted by Sahib Din, from a manuscript copy of the epic *Ramayana*, written in Sanskrit, from Udaipur (Rajasthan), AD 1652.

Add. 15297 (1), f. 29 a

Israfil, the Islamic angel of resurrection, blowing a trumpet to herald the Day of Judgment: from the 16th-century *'Aǧā'ib al-maḫlūqāt* (The Wonders of Nature) by Zakariyye ibn Muhammad al-Qazwīnī.

Or. 4701, f. 38v

Siyāvush riding through fire to prove his innocence after his stepmother, shown watching the scene from the building, had falsely accused him of treachery to his father. From a Persian manuscript dated 1486 of the *Shahnāma* (Book of Kings), the great epic poem of Iran, by Firdawsī. 22cm × 18cm

Add. 18188, f. 37v

Resident in Baghdad, was another important source of additions to the oriental collections in the 1870s.

In 1867, by which time the British Museum's holdings of oriental manuscripts amounted to 7000 volumes, the Department of Oriental Manuscripts was established as a sub-division of the Department of Manuscripts. In 1892, an entirely separate department was formed to administer both manuscripts and printed books in oriental languages. This was the Department of Oriental Printed Books and Manuscripts: the change to the more historically logical 'Oriental Manuscripts and Printed Books' came with the Department's incorporation into the British Library Reference Division in 1973.

Some 200 major languages, covering the whole of Asia and most of North and North-east Africa, which have a literary tradition, are now represented in the Department's collections. They also contain a rare heritage of artistic beauty, for the traditions of the Jewish, Christian, Islamic, Hindu and Buddhist religions and cultures are represented in manuscripts and books by exquisite illustrations as well as in words.

Delicately illuminated Hebrew codices from medieval France, Germany, Italy, Spain and Portugal; fine examples of Islamic art from Moorish Spain, Morocco, Egypt, the Middle East, Persia, Afghanistan and India; Persian painting in rich, courtly styles and the simpler provincial styles; and the art of Buddhist and Hindu India and South-east Asia may all be found in rich abundance in the Department's collections. Other South-east Asian countries well represented artistically include Burma, Thailand, Java and Bali; and from China and Japan in the Far East have come many fine examples of printing and calligraphy.

While these documents have been acquired primarily for their contents, their material form is also important, for it illustrates both the development of the book and the history of the written word. Manuscripts, charters and books may be written on papyrus or paper, vellum or silk, on palm-leaf, birch-bark, bone, ivory, copper plate and other metals, and on various kinds of cloth. They may be in codex form (i.e. like a normal book), or they may be scrolls, or folded concertina fashion, or even, as are one or two in the Department's collection, in the form of fans. Some are fragments so delicate that they require the most careful conservation and handling to be used at all.

As the Department of Oriental Manuscripts and Printed Books is very much a modern working library, it must expect its collections to receive considerable use. The Department maintains its own Conservation Workshop, where skilled specialists employing both modern scientific expertise and centuries-old techniques ensure that the bulk of the oriental holdings is readily available to readers in a manner which allows them to be handled without damage, while also preserving them intact for future users.

The Department serves the needs of scholars and others researching into all branches of the humanities and social sciences as they relate to the countries, peoples, and cultures of Asia and North Africa. The Oriental Reading Room seats forty people. It houses a reference collection, the current card catalogue, a complete set of published catalogues on open access and, since 1980, a multilingual microfiche catalogue; the rest of the collections are available on application.

To reinforce the continuing and regular supply of new items for its collections, the Department's senior staff visit their specialist language areas at intervals. Some 10,000 government publications from Asian countries come into the Department every year under official exchange schemes, and the Department itself subscribes to 4000 journals and a variety of oriental-language newspapers.

Many of the Department's catalogues have been the first and remain the most important bibliographic authorities in the world for the literature they cover. The first such, covering the collections of Syriac, Karshuni, Arabic and Ethiopic manuscripts, was published in three parts between 1838 and 1847. Since then, the practice has been to publish separate catalogues for each language, or group of languages.

The Department also regularly produces illustrated monographs on aspects of its collections, as well as illustrated guides to exhibitions mounted from time to time in the King's Library, where the Department's permanent exhibitions of treasures are also displayed.

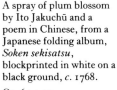

A spray of plum blossom by Ito Jakuchū and a poem in Chinese, from a Japanese folding album, *Soken sekisatsu*, blockprinted in white on a black ground, *c.* 1768.

Or. 64.a.11

The illuminated first word of the book of Deuteronomy, showing architectural motifs and grotesques, from the Duke of Sussex Pentateuch. This Hebrew manuscript from Germany dates from the 13th–14th century. 23cm × 16cm

Add. 15282, f. 238v

Women feeding a caged bird: a woodblock colour print by Utamaro from *Otoko-doka*, an anthology of Japanese comic poems published in 1798.

16099. c. 84.

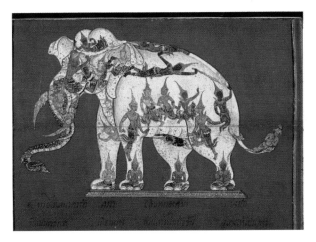

A 19th-century depiction from Thailand of the mythical 33-headed elephant flying through the sky as the vehicle of the god Indra.

Or. 13652, f. 7

The Israelites build cities for Pharaoh: a page from a 14th-century Spanish *Haggadah for the Eve of Passover*, an order of service that narrates the Exodus from Egypt. 25cm × 19cm

Add. 14761, f. 30v

67

A scene from a Turkish manuscript of the *Paşaname*, a poem celebrating the exploits of Ken'an Paşa (depicted here on horseback, listening to the pleas of peasants who have been suffering from the exactions of rebels). Painted in about 1630, there is a distinct western influence in the artist's approach, particularly in the perspective and the attention to factual detail.

Sloane 3584, f. 20a

Opposite: The title page of St John's Gospel from the *Awag Vank^c Gospels*. This classical Armenian text of the Four Gospels was copied in AD 1200–1 by the monk Vardan at the Awag monastery, near Erzincan on the upper Euphrates in Eastern Turkey, during the patriarchate of the Catholicos Gregory VI (1194–1203).

Or. 13654, f. 299r

Portrait of Colonel Colin Mackenzie,
Surveyor-General of India 1816–21, with
three Brahmin assistants. Oil painting by
Thomas Hickey painted at Madras in
1816.
F 13.

Below: A Hindu wedding ceremony.
Gouache painting of the Company School
by a Calcutta artist, 1798–1804.
Add Or 1121

INDIA OFFICE
LIBRARY AND RECORDS

The India Office Library and Records (IOLR), for whose collections the British Library became administratively responsible in 1982, is one of the world's oldest and most important research institutions, with a particular interest in South Asia. Its extensive holdings comprise two separate, though now jointly administered, collections, both of which grew out of the activities of the East India Company.

The Records, the elder of the two and part of the public records of the United Kingdom, date back to 1600, and are the surviving archives of the East India Company (1600–1858) and its successors as governors in the Indian sub-continent, the Board of Control (1784–1858), and the India Office (1858–1947) together with those of the Burma Office (1937–48).

In the Records can be traced the extraordinary history of the world's greatest trading company, of Britain's relationships with the lands and peoples of pre-independence India, and of the lives and work of British people in Asia, including those in the military and civil establishments. Although a considerable amount of material in the Records may also be found duplicated in various libraries, records offices and state institutions in India, the unique value of the collection in Orbit House lies both in its concentration of documentary material in one place and its supporting collections.

There are nearly 175,000 volumes, boxes and files of records, 11,000 volumes and boxes of European manuscripts, private papers, 70,000 official publications and 36,000 manuscript and printed maps, relating mainly to the countries of the Indian sub-continent (India, Pakistan, Bangladesh, Nepal, Sikkim and Bhutan). There is also much material from the huge section of the globe where the East India Company's charter gave it trading rights: from the borders of the Ottoman Empire to the southern tip of southern Africa, the Arabian Gulf states, Indonesia, Malaysia, Singapore, China, Japan and St Helena.

The Records contain an unbroken series of minutes of the East India Company's Court of Directors from 1600 to 1858, and the minutes of the Council of India, which succeeded it, to 1947. There are shelves of ships' journals and logs providing vivid and detailed pictures of shipboard life and of British trade with the East, and many volumes of letters, minutes and written exchanges between the Company and its 'factories' and packet and trading stations strung out over half the world, as well as with its three Presidencies – Madras, Bombay and Bengal – in India. Adding flesh to the skeleton of the archives, as it were, are many collections of the private papers of people who worked in India, from Viceroys and Governors General to the lowliest private in the Indian Army.

Still of considerable practical interest to many British people with Indian connections are the Ecclesiastical Records in which may be found the details of birth, marriage and death of many Christian Europeans in the East. The IOLR issues many hundreds of sealed certificates based on the Ecclesiastical Records every year.

The India Office Records, being part of the public records of the United Kingdom, as they relate to British connections with the Indian sub-continent and other Asian states, are held by permission of the Lord Chancellor and are subject to the provisions of Public Records Acts under which state papers are made available to the public.

The India Office Library, the younger of the two IOLR collections, was founded in 1801 as the Library of the Honourable East India Company to be a public repository for the oriental material, including many books and manuscripts, already in the Company's possession and a reference library for the Company's employees. Its first librarian, Sir Charles Wilkins, gained a formidable reputation as an oriental scholar and linguist, being the first European to acquire a thorough knowledge of Sanskrit and reveal to the Western world the vast range of Sanskrit literature. His work and that of other early orientalists, many of them the East India Company's administrators, judges and officials helped establish very early the Library's considerable reputation as a seat of oriental scholarship.

When the Crown took over the East India Company's powers in 1858 after the Mutiny, it also took over its assets and possessions, including the Library which became the successive responsibility of the India Office, the Commonwealth Relations Office, the Commonwealth Office and the Foreign and Commonwealth Office. The connection occurred by historical process rather than a combining of true interests, so that the recent transfer of responsibility for the administration and management of its collections and of the Records to the Board of the British Library seems both logical and appropriate. (Ownership of the IOLR is retained by the Secretary of State for Foreign and Commonwealth Affairs under a trust deed.) While India Office Library collections overlap in some areas with others in the British Library, they considerably enhance the latter's already outstanding Oriental collections.

The India Office Library is both an important reference library and a specialist library used by Asian scholars and Indologists all over the world. Its collection of printed books and serials in Western and

Oriental languages, the backbone of the Library, totals nearly 390,000 volumes. This number increases by several thousand annually under the Library's wide-ranging acquisitions policy (now co-ordinated with other departments in the British Library) which aims at obtaining all published work of any value, both classical and modern, in the languages of South Asia, of which the Library has about one hundred, and in Western languages relating to South Asia and to the other territories to which the interests of the East India Company and its successors extended.

Among the Library's 28,000 oriental manuscripts are many both unique and of considerable scholastic and artistic value. One curiosity which came from the famous oriental library of Tipu Sultan of Mysore, was a record of his dreams. The foundations of the collection were established in 1807 when the library puchased the oriental manuscripts and miniatures of Richard Johnson, an employee of the East India Company. Other important manuscript collections acquired early in its life by the Library included those of Warren Hastings, H. T. Colebrooke, Colin Mackenzie and F. Buchanan-Hamilton which also includes many natural history drawings. Sir Aurel Stein's archaeological expeditions to Central Asia at the beginning of this century uncovered large numbers of documents and manuscript fragments, many of which in Khotanese, Sanskrit and Tibetan were deposited in the India Office Library. (The complementary materials in Chinese are deposited in the Department of Oriental Manuscripts and Printed Books.)

The Library's newspaper and periodical collection, mostly in Western languages, is of particular interest to historians for it includes many early publications, a number of which have not survived elsewhere. For example, the Library has an almost complete run of *Hickey's Bengal Gazette* (1780–82), the first newspaper published in the subcontinent. However, the strength of the collection lies in its 19th-century publications.

The Library's prints and drawings collection, numbering more than 200,000 items, includes oil paintings, miniatures, drawings and photographs. Drawings and paintings in the Western style are by both Western and Indian artists, both professional and amateur, but all providing an invaluable record of topography and social life and of the natural history of the sub-continent. Many fine examples of oriental paintings may be found in the Library's collection of Persian and Indian miniatures.

The IOLR retains its own large conservation department, essential because of the great variety of materials – palm leaf, birch bark, wood, copper, silver, gold and ivory as well as paper and parchment – which may be found in the collections. It also has its own acquisitions policy, though this is now closely co-ordinated with other departments in the British Library.

The IOLR produces a large number of publications based on its collections, including guides, catalogues and illustrated monographs, now issued under The British Library imprint. A great scholarly undertaking just completed has been the publication of 'The Transfer of Power', a 12-volume series of official and unofficial documents edited by Professor Nicholas Mansergh covering the period leading up to India's independence, from 1942 to 15 August 1947.

The IOLR's collection may be consulted in its Reading Room, Map Room, Newspaper Library and Drawings Room at Orbit House in Blackfriars Road, London. Holders of British Library reader's tickets may use them for access to the IOLR, and day tickets may be obtained by other readers.

Opposite above: A watercolour view from the River Ganges of the Burning Ghats at Benares by Edward Lear, c. 1873. 16.6cm × 26.7cm
WD 2330

Opposite below: A gouache painting of a village scene in the Punjab, attributed to the Delhi artist Ghulam Ali Khan, c. 1820. 32cm × 43cm
Add. Or. 4057

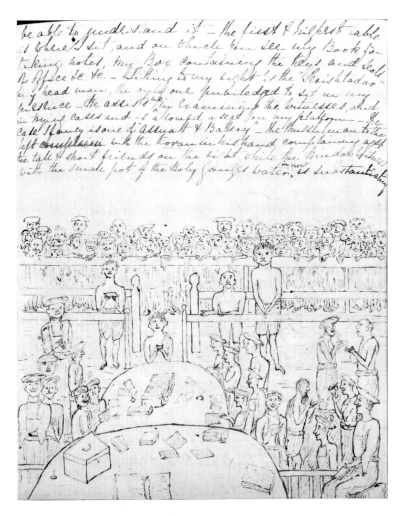

Hawkins Francis James, a magistrate in the Bengal Civil Service at Rangpur, made this pen and ink drawing of his court in his diary on 17 May 1836
MSS Eur B365

SCIENCE
REFERENCE LIBRARY

The Science Reference Library is this country's leading library for the natural sciences, engineering, technology and industrial property and also has an important role as a provider of information to business and commerce in Britain.

The SRL's beginnings may be traced in that flowering of engineering, technical and scientific skills in Victorian Britain which the Prince Consort harvested for his Great Exhibition in 1851.

At this time, there was no one coherent system for recording and registering patents. Reform, for which manufacturers and inventors had long been campaigning, came in 1852 with the passing of the Patent Law Amendment Act, the major provision of which was the establishment of Commissioners of Patents who would administer a new Patent Office.

Bennet Woodcroft, a former Manchester manufacturer and inventor, a member of the Society of Arts, and Professor of Descriptive Machinery at University College, London since 1847, was appointed Assistant to the Commissioners with special responsibility for specifications of patents.

Iris persica: the first plate in *The Botanical Magazine; or Flower-Garden Displayed*, published in London for W. Curtis in 1787. Science Reference Library.

By the end of 1852 Woodcroft, well-established at the new Patent Office at 25 Southampton Buildings, Holborn, was already planning to open a public library where the specifications of patented inventions, as well as books and materials from Britain and abroad 'indispensable to the right direction and advance of British industry' might be readily available for consultation. In March 1855, the Patent Office Library, the direct ancestor of SRL, was opened. From the outset, the Library kept all its stock on open access, the first public library in the UK to do so, and still today allows direct access to as high a proportion as space will permit. The SRL is the only department of the British Library's Reference Division for which intending users do not need passes or special reader's tickets.

The Patent Office Library's 'foundation collections' were the private libraries collected by Woodcroft and by a Birmingham engineer, Richard Prosser. These were initially lent to the Patent Office Library then later bought by the Commissioner of Patents. To these two libraries were added the publications of the British Patent Office, also used then, as now, for international exchange agreements, and donations from individual companies and authors.

Under Woodcroft, the Patent Office embarked on a rapid retrospective programme of publishing patent specifications, and in six years had published more than 14,000 British specifications and their drawings, dating from 1618 to 1852, plus Woodcroft's own records and indexes. The Library grew rapidly and by the time Woodcroft retired in 1876 Victorian businessmen, engineers and inventors had free use of the greatest technical library in Europe.

In 1951, an Advisory Council on Scientific Policy proposed that two national science libraries should be formed, one for lending (now the British Library's Lending Division at Boston Spa), and one for reference. However, it was not until 1960, when the British Museum was given the task of creating a National Reference Library of Science and Invention (NRLSI), that things really began to move on the latter.

Responsibility for the Patent Office Library was transferred to the British Museum in 1966, and the old reading room in the Patent Office building became the Holborn division of the NRLSI. New accommodation had to be found to house the growing collection of literature on the non-inventive sciences and technologies.

With the establishment of the British Library in 1973, the NRLSI, now re-named the Science Reference Library, was incorporated into the British Library's Reference Division. The SRL sees its primary purpose as being to contribute to the economic progress of the UK by encouraging and facilitating the exploitation of published scientific, technical and related information. To this end it makes its reference collection easily accessible to research workers from industry. For these people, and for many others across the spectrum of industry and science – information officers, scientific writers and journalists, industrial managers, librarians, patent and trade mark agents – SRL is both a 'first resort' and 'last resort' library.

SRL's collections include more than 50,000 serial titles, 170,000 books and monographs, well over 20 million patent specifications from those countries all round the world which publish their patents, and over 2 million items on microform. SRL has also put on microform the catalogue of all its acquisitions since 1975 and much of the earlier material.

The collections are uniquely comprehensive. Their holdings on the development of the photography of the earth's surface from above, for instance, extends from Gaspard Felix Tournachon's patented invention for aerial photography from balloons in 1858, up to indexes and listings of recent image data obtained from the LANDSAT satellite programmes.

SRL's collections are constantly being added to, with about 8000 books and monographs, well over 200,000 serial parts and over 900,000 patent specifications coming into the Library every year. Each week's new British and European patents can be seen immediately they are published every Wednesday and are the subject of intense interest from the moment the Library opens. The latest foreign patents are obtained by the quickest means so that they are available at SRL as soon as possible after publication.

In response to demand from industry and from other libraries, the SRL has recently extended its coverage of business-related literature and, based on this, now offers its Business Information Service.

Apart from the services available direct to readers in its three London reading rooms, SRL also operates extensive services for those unable to visit. It accepts enquiries by telephone, telex and post, and its staff can check references and trace sources of scientific information for callers.

SRL's Computer Search Service gives access to a wide range of computer-based bibliographic services and factual data banks in Britain and abroad, including undertaking patent family searches, providing the technical details of related patents in various languages, including Japanese and Russian. Staff will also translate into English the short titles of, or other extracts from, documents, thus helping readers to decide if material in a foreign language is likely to be useful to them.

SRL produces bibliographies, guides to particular services or collections and introductory guides to individual subjects. It has two regular newsletters: *SRL news*, giving the latest information on new services, developments and publications, and *PIN Bulletin*, in association with the other libraries of the UK Patents Information Network (PIN).

Opposite: The Science Reference Library's galleried reading room at 25 Southampton Buildings, designed by Sir John Taylor, was opened to readers in 1902

Details from US patent 3,138,743, for which application was made in February 1959. This is the silicon 'chip', whose invention by Jack S. Kilby has made possible the microcomputer. Science Reference Library.

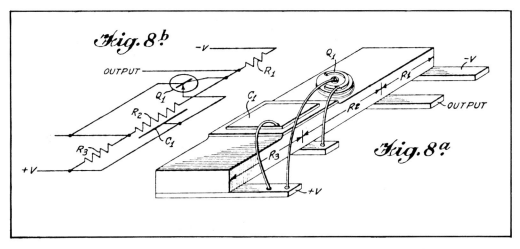

SELECT BIBLIOGRAPHY

Books about the British Library and its collections:

The British Museum Library by Arundell Esdaile. 1944, 2nd. imp. 1948 (out of print, but still available from libraries)

Prince of Librarians. The Life and Times of Antonio Panizzi of the British Museum by Edward Miller. 1967

That Noble Cabinet: A History of the British Museum by Edward Miller. 1973

The Reading Room by P. R. Harris. 1979

The British Library: guide to the catalogues and indexes of the Department of Manuscripts by M. A. E. Nickson. 2nd ed., 1982

Guide to the Department of Oriental Manuscripts and Printed Books by J. H. Goodacre and A. P. Pritchard. 1977

Guide to the India Office Library, with a note on the India Office Records by S. C. Sutton. 2nd ed., 1971

The British Library publishes many books relating to the Library collections. These may be purchased in the Bernard Shaw Shop in the British Museum, or by post from Publications Sales Unit, The British Library, Boston Spa, Wetherby, W. Yorkshire LS23 7BQ. Please write for a complete catalogue.

Written by Janice Anderson
Designed by Peter Campbell

© 1983 The British Library Board

Reprinted, with corrections 1985

Published by
The British Library
Reference Division Publications
Great Russell Street
London WC1B 3DG

British Library Cataloguing in Publication Data
   Anderson, Janice
      The British Library Reference Division collections.
      1. British Library. *Reference Division*
      I. Title
      027.541   Z675.N2
ISBN 0-7123-0009-0

Typeset by Tradespools Ltd., Frome, Somerset
Printed in England by Balding & Mansell Ltd., Wisbech